The Place of the Mourning Doves

Reaching Out to Romanian Orphans

Karleen Dewey

Ampelos Press
Drexel Hill, PA

ISBN 978-0-9661305-8-4

Published by Ampelos Press for
Mercy Ministries of Colorado
PO 140597
Edgewater, CO 80214

Scripture quotations noted KJV are from the King James Version.

Scripture quotations marked (NASB) are from the New American Standard Bible®
Copyright © 1960, 1962, 1963, 1968, 1971, 1972, 1973, 1975, 1977, 1995 by
The Lockman Foundation. Used by permission. (www.Lockman.org)

Scripture quotations marked (NIV) are taken from the Holy Bible, NEW INTERNATIONAL VERSION®. Copyright © 1973, 1978, 1984 International Bible Society. All rights reserved throughout the world. Used by permission of International Bible Society. NEW INTERNATIONAL VERSION® and NIV® are registered trademarks of International Bible Society. Use of either trademark for the offering of goods or services requires the prior written consent of International Bible Society.

Quote from Sheraz Khurram Khanof on page 29 used by permission of ASSIST News Service. (http://www.assistnews.net)

Quotes from Izidor Ruckel on pages 137 and 141 from *Abandoned for Life* (St. Louis: J.B. Information Station, 2002). Used by permission. (http://www.abandonedforlife.com and http://www.EmpoweredParent.com)

Cover design and art by Ben Dewey

Inside design and editing by Marlene Bagnull

Inside art by Jocelyn Davis

Photography provided by Loving Arms Team

Printed in the United States of America

Dedication

To my children
Scott
Kathy
Kim
Kris
Karyn
Jon
Shane
Josie
Christine
Wendi
who have taught me much.

"Can a mother forget the baby at her breast
And have no compassion on the child
she has borne?
Though she may forget,
I will not forget you!"

Isaiah 49:15 NIV

table of contents

Acknowledgments

This is not the whole story. It is only the story from my viewpoint. Volumes would be needed to relate all the experiences and ups and downs the volunteers and staff have experienced while ministering to the orphans in this one little corner of Romania.

However, none of these experiences would have happened without some key people. My heroes are Barbro and Lars Gustavsson. He is a man of vision and she a woman of prayer. Together, with their dedication and perseverance, they helped make dreams for the orphans come true. Dan and Lidia Micula were dedicated to the children from the start. They have been my sounding board and are my teachers of Romanian culture. Florin and Camelia Costea gave up good professional jobs to come and serve in leadership roles with Fundatia Crestina Elim (FCE). Florin has worked through many problems and issues to bring hope to abandoned children. Both couples have shared their lives with us and made us feel at home.

The faces of many volunteers float before my eyes. Some have shared their stories with me. I thank them for the love and care they continue to give the orphans. I credit them for many of the successes with the children. Together we have worked and struggled through difficulties. In witnessing their faith in action, I have been encouraged in my own. Many volunteers have spent years in Marghita ministering to the children under FCE. All of them had a significant impact on the orphans, and I am truly grateful for their contributions. I wish I could recognize each one by name. They are the "cream of the crop."

I have many people to thank. Foremost, is my editor, Marlene Bagnull, who said "This story should be told." She helped me with every detail of the manuscript. My family and friends gave their wholehearted support even when I had to give up time with them to write. Our oldest son, Scott, and his wife, Melanie, have shared many of our experiences in Romania and contributed to this book with fresh insights.

Every grandmother is proud of her grandchildren. Ben Dewey used his talents in computer graphics to design a creative cover. Jocelyn Davis has artistic talent way beyond her years. Her drawings appear inside the book. Mary Dewey is gifted in writing and expressed her compassion for the children in her essays in the appendix. I hope someday she will write a book from the viewpoint of a teen whose outlook on life was changed through her relationships with the orphans.

Diane Pulvermiller, Barb Demolar, and Phyllis Parker are my friends who frequently go to Romania to give their hearts to the children. I thank them for adding their passionate stories to this book. Dr. Inger Bostrom gave me my first glimpse of the orphans in Marghita. Our "chance" meeting in 1991 has led to a lifelong ministry partnership and friendship. Two very important men, Jim Vincent of Lakewood, Colorado, and Zoli Szabo of Marghita, Romania, spent many hours keeping my computers running. Without them this book would not have been finished on time.

Then there are the children who shared some of their heartbreak with me. They gifted me with their trust and told me stories they understood would be printed for the world to read. To protect them, I have not always used their real names.

My first editor before I sent any chapter to Marlene was my husband, Fred. Together, we were called to go to Romania to minister to the children. I cherish our lives together these past five decades. He is my soul mate and a wonderful man of God who adds much wisdom to my life. I love him more each day.

Fred Dewey and orphans

Foreword

Today, at the breakfast table, my eye caught a line in our newspaper referring to a certain destination "where every single moment is another opportunity to live an unforgettable experience." The blurb was contained in an advertisement for a resort which is a true "paradise" for those able to afford it.

I could not help but think of the many, many places where I have been privileged to live unforgettable experiences—but at the other end of the lengthy continuum that stretches from the "Shangri-la" of human thinking to what many would freely call "hell on earth."

We live on a planet where the contrast between the "haves" and the "have-nots" is truly dramatic. Many of us, however, find it convenient to close our eyes and our hearts to those victims of war, crime, poverty, corruption, and extreme deprivation of every kind. What we mostly take for granted in our American suburbs is in short supply in much of the so-called Third World. It is difficult to comprehend a world where a quarter of a million children under the age of five die every week of easily cured maladies—if only there were those who cared enough.

We consider "blessed" those financially able to enjoy wonderful travel destinations catering to the comforts of the physical senses. It is not easy to think that the truly "blessed" are those who enter into the ghettos, the slums, the prisons, the war-torn countries, and the hospitals to share the burdens of the victims of a throw-away culture. But the truly worthwhile "unforgettable experiences" are those in the world's "hell holes" where, by God's grace and strength, we've been able to make a difference in the lives of a few. The reason is contained in the simple words of Jesus: "I was hungry and you gave me something to eat, I was thirsty and you gave me something to drink, I was a stranger and you invited me in, I needed clothes and you clothed me, I was sick and you looked after me, I was in prison and you came to visit me . . . Whatever you did for one of the least of these brothers of mine, you did for me" (Matt. 25:35–36, 40 NIV).

As I picked up the manuscript of Karleen Dewey's book that you now hold in your hand, I reflected quickly on my relationship with this family, a relationship now that is close to forty years old. Fred and Karleen, with their children, moved into a house across the street from where I lived, and they began to attend the church where I was the pastor. At that time, of course, I had no idea that regardless of whatever ministry I would have to them, they would have a greater ministry to me and to my family—a ministry beyond the time and space to detail here.

I was destined to find out that here were people with a characteristic that is eminently Christ-like—the quality of compassion. Out of that deep reservoir of simple caring, a Vietnamese baby, a Filipino street boy, and a Mexican-Indian girl were adopted, and Mercy Ministries was birthed. At first this was a compassionate caring for mothers and their children in the inner city, where the lack of resources and education created an enormous need. It eventually spread to ministry in the Philippines, and then to the neglected, often-abandoned, children of Romania. That is where this story begins.

At a time in life when many of us think of taking things easy, enjoying the fruit of our years of labor, relishing the joy of being around our happy grandchildren, Fred and Karleen Dewey ventured to Eastern Europe to take on a major responsibility for abandoned and deprived children. Their efforts to make a difference in the lives of these neglected children makes fascinating reading.

There are books that demand reading—not because they are so enjoyable, but because they tell a story that needs to be shouted from the rooftops. This is one of them. The resources in our American churches are enormous, but they will be tapped only if the spirit of deep compassion, which moved the Deweys, is somehow infused into more of our church members. Here is a book that is interesting and informative, but beyond that, demonstrates what a few of God's people are capable of accomplishing with faith, determination, and the willingness to be used by the Spirit of God.

My hope and prayer is not that the reader will merely become aware of the children of Romania, but that the godly spirit of compassion will move more of God's people to seize opportunities to have unforgettable experiences among the many deprived and hurting people—about whom God cares so much. For, when all is said and done: "Blessed are the merciful, for they shall receive mercy" (Matt. 5:7 NASB).

DR. JAMES MEANS, Senior Professor
Denver Seminary - Denver, Colorado

Introduction

Transylvania . . . land of mystery and intrigue. Castles, Dracula, secret police . . . The country of Romania conjures up many imaginative and evil images. Some images are authentic, while others are purely fictitious.

Transylvania, the region of western Romania running east to the Carpathian Mountains, is truly magnificent. Driving through the lowlands, the visitor is treated to lovely pastoral scenes with peasants and farm animals. Grannies dressed in widow's black garb sit on benches in front of doorways scrutinizing the local activities. Stucco houses with red-tiled roofs add charm to the villages. Now and then a stork lands in her nest on top of a telephone pole. Geese and ducks scuttling across the road somehow miss getting hit by speeding cars.

Lacking sunlight, the impenetrable Black Forest and rushing streams give way to breathtaking mountains. Bedecked with wildflowers, mountain plateaus open to another world of sheer beauty. A sense of wildness and peace resides here. Sheep and shepherds with shaggy sheepskin coats lounge in the meadow grass. In the distance, the higher snowcapped Carpathians reign over this land in Eastern Europe.

Lest we are lulled into a vision of tranquility, all too recent memories of the dictator Ceausescu and the Securitate come to mind. For decades this crazy man and his henchmen wreaked havoc on Romania. His insidious master plan of creating twenty-three million factory workers unraveled the very fabric of the country—the family and the village. He plowed over hundreds of villages, replacing them with ugly concrete apartment buildings which are crumbling day by day.

The family support system weakened as extended families were separated. Working long hours for scant wages became the norm. Ceausescu set into motion a plan for each family to have five or more children. Modern health care was nonexistent and adequate food in short supply. Waiting in long lines to buy basic necessities increased the frustration of the Romanian people. Today, Romanian families continue to suffer. Alcoholism is widespread. Inflation has skyrocketed. Food and other necessities are available now, but many families cannot afford them.

The greatest tragedy was the devaluation of human life. Thousands of children were abandoned to state orphanages. Babies were left at the hospitals while their mothers quietly slipped away. Children who grew up in an orphanage were severely neglected and as a consequence were emotionally troubled and delayed in all areas of their development. As a result, they do not have the vocational skills necessary to make a living. Generations of Romanians will be affected before the extreme poverty of soul and spirit will be healed.

> *The greatest tragedy*
> *was the devaluation of human life.*
> *Thousands of children were abandoned*
> *to state orphanages.*

Following his execution in December of 1989, pictures of the dead Ceausescu lying in a pool of blood ran constantly on television. Jubilant Romanians celebrated in the streets. Many thought Romania would quickly return to normalcy. The fall of communism opened the doors for change, but change in any country comes slowly.

Years later, about one-fourth of Romanians still live below the poverty line. The average salary is about two hundred and fifty dollars per month. The depressing truth is available funds are not sufficient to provide for the country's disenfranchised—the disabled, widows, single mothers, and orphans.

> *Generations of Romanians will be affected*
> *before the extreme poverty of soul*
> *and spirit will be healed.*

For sixteen years, my husband and I have been in and out of Romania teaching orphanage staff to care for abandoned children. In 1986, Fred and I founded Mercy Ministries, a nonprofit organization with programs for poor, neglected, and abandoned children in Denver and the Philippines, expanding the ministry in 1991 to Romania. Under *Project Loving Arms*, a team of fifteen to twenty volunteers travels to Romania each summer to care for the abandoned babies and run camps for older orphans.

The Romanian Christian foundation, Fundatia Crestina Elim (FCE), coordinates the work of an international team of Romanians, Swedes, Americans, Brits, and Canadians who live and work in Marghita year around to care for the children.

Romanians are gracious and hospitable, and I enjoy them very much. They have a wonderful sense of humor and are fun-loving. Sometimes I forget that under communism they suffered terrible hardships.

One pastor said, "Oh, you can't imagine what it was like. No, you could never imagine . . . When the trucks of humanitarian goods came into the country, people had not seen a banana and did not know to peel it before you eat it."

Emerging from years of poverty and deprivation, Romania could not change overnight. Yet I have seen great changes. The roads are no longer full of potholes. The towns and villages have streetlights. Tramlines have been repaired, and efficient inter-city trains speed people along in comfort.

> *Emerging from years of poverty and deprivation,*
> *Romania could not change overnight.*
> *Yet I have seen great changes.*

The change in thinking about the welfare of children is a bit slower in coming. New laws meant to safeguard the children are in place. New generations are seeing the need to protect Romania's greatest resource . . . its children.

It is my hope that mothers will no longer abandon their children. However, because of poverty, prejudice, and a lack of understanding of the severe consequences of neglect, beautiful babies continue to be abandoned at an alarming rate. My deep conviction is that every child deserves a family. My vision is a family for every child, and the foundation is working to see that vision become a reality. In the meantime, "loving arms" will continue to reach out to these needy orphans.

> *Let those*
> *who think I have said too little*
> *and those who think I have said too much,*
> *forgive me;*
> *and let those who think I have said just enough*
> *thank God with me.*
> **St. Augustine**

So Close

They can see the light,
Just of out of sight.
They can feel the love,
Just out of reach.

I see their bright hopes,
Only to realize their dark fears.

I can hear faint pleas,
Answered by loud refusals.

I feel their soft love,
Giving way to sharp hate.

I taste their sweet freedom,
Replaced by bitter imprisonment.

They can see the light,
Just of out of sight.
They can feel the love,
Just out of reach.

Ben Dewey, age 16

Place of the Mourning Doves

There were those who dwelt in darkness and
in the shadow of death, prisoners in misery and chains.

Psalm 107:10 NASB

On another cold day in March of 1998 I pause to sit on a rusty bench in the courtyard outside the pediatric section of the hospital in Marghita, Romania.

I am drawn again and again to this place where it all began many years ago. High above, doves perched on bare branches silhouette against the sky. I struggle with my emotions as I hear their somber call. To me, they are mourning for the lost children who are imprisoned inside the hospital. "Cooo, Cooo, Cooo." Now, whenever I hear that poignant sound, my thoughts return to my first encounter with Romanian orphans.

A large, brown stucco building, Marghita Hospital shows no outward change since my first visit in 1991. Memories flood my mind. A baby with thin arms grasping my finger. Dark eyes searching my face. The stench of urine from ragged cloth diapers and soaked horsehair mattresses. Bare gray-green walls. Chain link metal cribs with chipped white paint that serve as cages for the children.

I remember one morning standing with a feverish baby in my arms. I closed my eyes and imagined a pitiful wail coming out of my mouth. In my mind I allowed myself to scream: *How can you treat babies like animals? How can you starve them? How dare you not hold them?* My anger mounted. *I'll open the windows and throw out these filthy mattresses. I'll rip out the toilet that doesn't flush and the faucets that give only cold water. I'll throw out the gruel you feed the toddlers. I will take these babies out of this damnable place.* My angry outburst subsided as I imagined escaping from this hellhole with the babies.

In reality, my angry screams remained bottled up within me. Venting my rage, although cathartic for me, would only have worsened the plight of these babies. A hopeless future awaited these children, but I was determined to do something for them.

> *What was I doing in Romania anyway?*
> *My home is in a comfortable suburb*
> *of Denver, Colorado. My grandchildren are quick*
> *to give hugs and kisses and good-bye waves.*

My home is in a comfortable suburb of Denver, Colorado. My grandchildren are quick to give hugs and kisses and good-bye waves. I delight in playing patty-cake with giggly babies. At the first sign of a fever, these children are rushed to see a pediatrician. The mothers I know love and nurture their babies.

In October of 1990, ABC's 20/20 program aired an expose' of the nightmarish living conditions for thousands of Romanian orphans. My husband, Fred, and I watched in silence. Tears rolled down my cheeks. My heart ached. Fred and I looked at each other. Finally Fred said, "I think we should go." I nodded in agreement.

> *In October of 1990, ABC's 20/20 program*
> *aired an expose' of the nightmarish living conditions*
> *for thousands of Romanian orphans.*
> *Fred said, "I think we should go."*

After searching our world map, we located Romania in Eastern Europe. Going to Europe would be a new experience. Our adult children were proud that we were going to Romania to help the orphans. They knew we were experienced with abandoned children. Our family fostered seven children from infants to teens. We made food boxes for unemployed families and looked after young single mothers. We raised our children to love and serve Jesus Christ and to go wherever they were called by God to go.

God Prepared Us to Be Risk Takers

Our large family has a history of doing the unusual. As I look back through the years, I can see where God prepared us to be risk takers. I do not feel like a courageous person, but I seem to take on the challenge of adventure. In the 1970s my dream was to homestead in the Alaskan wilderness. Though we did not move to Alaska, we did take our then family of five young children on a five-week tent camping trip to Alaska.

In 1975, after the fall of Saigon, we adopted a Vietnamese baby. Later, we adopted a nine-year-old Filipino street boy and a six-year-old Mexican-Indian girl. In 1984-85, Fred took a teaching sabbatical and we moved our family to Manila for a year. In the Philippines, we added a three-year-old girl to our family. Thus, our family grew to ten children.

Mothering the Unmothered

Several of our adopted children experienced abuse and abandonment prior to being placed with us. With a university degree in early childhood development, I developed a strong interest in attachment issues of orphans. For years, I lived with adopted children who often fought against the close, loving relationships offered in our family. I took every graduate course I could and read dozens of books relating to reactive attachment disorder, or RAD. Because of my academic background and life experiences, I felt qualified to teach others how to "mother the unmothered." In 1990, I was invited to the Philippines to teach a seminar to orphanage caregivers. The seminar was applauded as a significant turning point in the way the orphanage caregivers nurtured the children in their care.

With all these experiences behind us, Fred and I prepared to go to Romania believing we had something of value to give to those who care for the orphans. I did not question my ability to teach valuable information, but I did question whether it would be well received. Would Romanians welcome new ways to care for the orphans?

Even though our adult children were highly in favor of our going to Romania, not all of our relatives were. Fred's mother wrote from her home in western New York that she wished we would not go. Fred's father and mother had spent many years informing others of the evils of communism. She was aware that a country does not change overnight, and she felt we would be in danger. In going to Romania, we would be stepping through a former Iron Curtain. Fred tried to reassure her that we would be safe. Nothing he said ever changed her mind.

Deep down I felt God called us to go, but I also felt a nagging uncertainty for our safety.

Deep down I felt God called us to go, but I also felt a nagging uncertainty for our safety. I also worried about the cost of the trip. We had enough frequent flyer miles for tickets to Munich, Germany. When friends who lived in Augsburg, Germany, and Vienna, Austria, graciously offered us places to stay, we gladly accepted. Fred, a chemistry professor, was teaching an accelerated chemistry course early in the summer and then had a break before the fall semester began. We had three weeks to travel to Romania.

Once we announced we were going, friends from our church in Lakewood, Colorado, wanted to help with our expenses. Suddenly, people began to contact us who either knew a Romanian or an American who had recently traveled to Romania. We gleaned as much advice as we could from them. To conform to the cultural dress in Romanian churches, I packed a head scarf and blouses with sleeves. I bought some dark skirts and left my jewelry at home. I knew I would be meeting people who had few material possessions. I planned to dress simply to avoid standing out in any way.

In July of 1991, we started on our journey to Romania knowing little of what awaited us. We had the name of a Swedish pastor, Lars Hornberg, living in Oradea, Romania, who wanted to start a Christian orphanage. In June, we had met a Romanian doctor, Rodica Urziceanu, who was visiting Denver. When she heard we planned to go to Romania, she invited us to come to Bucharest to visit some orphanages. Lars and Rodica were our only two contacts. We were told that we should meet the pastors of a large Baptist church in Oradea. Many unknowns lay before us. We did not know where we would stay or how to find out about the condition of the orphans.

We did not know where we would stay or how to find out about the condition of the orphans.

We flew from Denver to JFK airport in New York. We had a short time between our flights, so we had to hurry to the gates for international flights. It was a challenge to keep our passports and papers ready to show at any moment. Our next stop was Munich where missionary friends, Jonas and Sadie Stolzfus, greeted us. We had corresponded for years and enjoyed our short overnight visit in their home. Sadie was known for her "Pennsylvania Dutch" hospitality and made us feel like family. Fluent in German, Jonas arranged for train tickets and saw that we found the right train to Vienna the next morning.

Our longtime Colorado friends, Duane and Janice Mullet, lived in Vienna where Duane worked for the UN. Janice cooked us delicious tacos . . . true western "comfort food." Duane is a jokester and kept us laughing as he told about life in Vienna. I could feel my tense muscles slowly relax for the first time in days. But the tone of our evening together changed as Janice and Duane expressed concern about our plans to travel to Romania, a country they still considered unsafe for western travelers.

Despite ominous warnings . . .

When Romania's dictator, Nicolae Ceausescu, was executed in December of 1989, he left the country in disarray and turmoil. The rates of unemployment and inflation were high, food was scarce, and the Romanian people were suffering. The Securitate, the dreaded state secret police, were still around observing the comings and goings of the people. Even with these ominous warnings, we were determined to go and see what we could do to help the orphans.

Our trial by fire was about to begin.

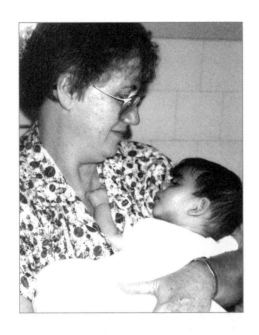

A hopeless future awaited these children, but I was determined to do something for them.

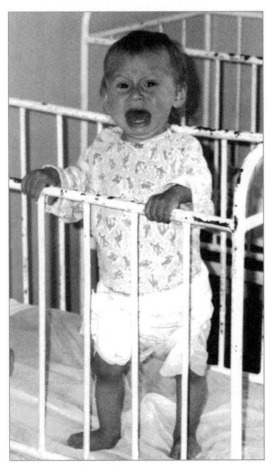

2

Trial by Fire

Consider it all joy, my brethren, when you encounter various trials,
knowing that the testing of your faith produces endurance.

James 1:2-3 NASB

Feeling a sudden jerk and pull on my shoulder bag, I wheeled around only to see a man laughing at me. Our friend, Duane, had escorted us to the Vienna train station. In an attempt to warn me to be careful and to illustrate my vulnerability, he sneaked up behind me and pulled my bag off my shoulder. My apprehension went up a notch.

As we boarded the train in Vienna for Budapest, a queasy feeling of impending disaster hit me. Was God warning us? Why did I feel it now as Fred and I were about to find ourselves exactly where God called us to be . . . in Romania? Perhaps I was just nervous about changing train stations in a big city where we could not speak the language or read the signs. I prayed that if we had trouble finding where to go, we would meet someone who could speak English and direct us.

After arriving in Budapest, we took a taxi from the Keleti train station to the Nyugati station where we were to catch the train to Romania. I kept thinking, *What if the taxi driver takes us somewhere and robs us?* To me, the driver looked like a "tough" in a red muscle shirt pulled tightly over his chest. He was the first Hungarian I met. Stiffly, I sat in the backseat of the cab praying that we were heading for Nyugati station. Totally oblivious of the beautiful city of Budapest, I stared at the driver's back.

Upon arriving at the Nyugati station, we moved our bags inside. While Fred checked the train schedule, I leaned against a wall clutching my purse and keeping a watchful eye on our bags. Fred returned to say the train for Romania was leaving in ten minutes, so we grabbed our bags and hurried to the platform to find our car. War raged to the south in Yugoslavia, and I didn't want to accidentally end up there.

Steady rain drenched the platform as we moved to our car. Gripping the metal handrail, I pulled myself up the steps and into the car. Fred followed with our bags. I chose a seat next to the window in a nonsmoking section and sat down, heaving a big sigh of relief. Fred and I smiled at each other, and I said, "We did it! That wasn't so bad." I surveyed our surroundings. The car seats were clean and comfortable. For the moment, my fears seemed unfounded.

For the moment, my fears seemed unfounded.

Minutes later, I reached for the black zipper bag we were carrying. I couldn't find it! "Fred, where is the zipper bag?" All the names and telephone numbers of Romanian contacts and our airline tickets were in the bag. We franticly looked around us.

"We have to get off and find it," Fred said.

Rushing off the train, I cried, "We can't go if we don't have the bag."

Fred gently pushed me against the wall of the train station. As the rain soaked us, he put his arms around me and prayed. "God, help us find our bag. Help us get to Romania."

We retraced our steps through the station, but the bag was nowhere.

We retraced our steps through the station, but the bag was nowhere. The same taxi driver with the muscle shirt waited for customers outside. We told him what happened and looked on the floor in the back of the taxi. He checked his trunk and then sighed. "Gypsies." For him, one word explained our plight. He seemed a bit kinder as he drove us back to Keleti station. To our disappointment, Keleti station did not have a lost and found window.

"What are we going to do?" I kept saying, trying not to cry. "All those folks back home are supporting us, and we will disappoint them."

"We have come this far," Fred said firmly. "We must go on to Romania."

I no longer felt a knot of fear.
It was now the kind of fear that paralyzes.

Discouraged, we took a taxi back to Nyugati station to catch a later train heading east for Romania. This train was not as streamlined as the first train. As we boarded, we were struck by the dirty, shabby condition of the car both inside and out. I no longer felt a knot of fear. It was now the kind of fear that paralyzes.

No conductor greeted us as we climbed up the steps of our car. The floor of the train was sloppy, apparently with scrub water. Avoiding the puddles, we found a private compartment. Each side of the compartment had three seats which faced those on the other side. At one time, the threadbare red upholstery might have been luxurious. Now broken springs left the middle seats several inches higher than the others. Any thoughts of a comfortable nap quickly faded when I stretched out across the seats. As the train jostled along, the compartment door swung back and forth. The latch was broken.

Don't worry; I am the lifter of your head. You must eat.

The summer of 1991 was a wet one for Eastern Europe. Through the grimy windows, I saw rain falling on fields already saturated with water. Stunted corn stalks stood drowning in the fields. Shallow lakes divided by fences dotted the landscape. The Hungarian countryside looked like blobs of muted green and brown on an artist's pallet.

Our traumatic afternoon turned to evening. Fred and I had not eaten all day although we had bought sandwiches for lunch in the train station before leaving Vienna. My sandwich was tasteless and dry in my mouth, and I could not eat it. As I lay across the seats, shifting my position to try to get comfortable, I heard a voice in my head. *Don't worry; I am the lifter of your head. You must eat.* It was as though God said, "Here, take this bread and eat." I sat up and gobbled down my sandwich. The lyrics of a song flowed through my mind. "Thank You, Father," I prayed. "You're the lifter of my head."

Our train rumbled east passing through formerly communist-controlled lands.

Our train rumbled east passing through formerly communist-controlled lands. Deserted collective farm buildings slouched at various angles. In village after village the scene was the same: red-roofed stucco houses and soggy vegetable gardens. Women wobbled along on rickety bicycles through the muddy streets. An old man limped through the rain with a large, unwrapped loaf of bread under his arm.

The train ride from Budapest eastward through Hungary to the Romanian border dragged on for hours. Just as my children asked so many times, I asked myself, *When will we ever get there?* Once in Oradea, I had hopes that we could contact the train line to ask about a lost and found department. In my American mind-set, I thought all would be orderly once we climbed off the train.

As we came to the Hungarian-Romanian border, my anxiety increased. "A mean border to cross," our friends had warned us. Anything could happen. Our train squeaked to a stop in an area completely void of trees. There were no signs of life other than the armed border guards. My mind quickly flashed to visions of barbed wire, vicious barking dogs, and desperate people attempting to escape. Instinctively I knew we were in "no-man's-land."

As recently as two years before, Romanians had tried to flee across this strip of land into Hungary in search of a better life. The penalty for getting caught was death or even worse . . . every bone broken in the poor soul's body. A shiver ran down my spine as I looked out over the barren landscape.

The grayness of the evening faded to blackness. We sat in silence. No sunset settled over Eastern Europe. No lights came on inside the train or outside. I whispered nervously to Fred, "What are they waiting for?"

The grayness of the evening faded to blackness.

An hour passed. Some of the other passengers leaned out open train windows trying to see something. Then I heard several men board the train. Flashlight beams flitted about as they walked through our car. As the men approached, I tensed when I saw their uniforms and guns. I felt as if a boulder were lodged in my stomach. With a grim face one of the men barked, "Passport!" We handed our passports to him and were shocked when he walked away with them. "Always keep your passport in sight," was our rule for foreign travel.

Another hour passed . . . in total darkness. Were we at the border? Every muscle in my body tightened. My jaw clenched and my mouth went dry. In my heightened state of fear, I imagined the worst scenarios. Would we ever see our passports or another dawn? Suddenly, I heard the heavy boots of the uniformed men. One man stopped at our compartment and returned our stamped passports. What a relief!

Would we ever see our passports or another dawn?

The train lurched forward and once again we began to move eastward into Romania. In the absence of a conductor or a train schedule, we did not know how long it would take to arrive at our destination. We understood Oradea was a sizable city and would be the first stop past the border. After about fifteen minutes, the train stopped at a station, but which station? In the faint light from the station windows, my eyes strained to see a sign identifying the station.

An approaching train stopped on the tracks between our train and the station. The glaring headlight of the oncoming engine revealed workmen repairing the tracks. I leaned out an open window and yelled, "Oradea?" One of the workmen answered "Da." What "da" meant I didn't know. We felt we should take our chances and get off the train.

Grabbing our bags, we cautiously picked our way across the tracks guided by the headlight of the other train.

Inside the station various shadowy figures leaned against the walls. In the dim, yellow light diffused by cigarette smoke everything appeared eerie. I looked around for an information window hoping to find someone who could tell us in English where we were. Through one open window I saw a sleepy-looking woman sitting in a chair.

"Oradea?" I asked.

I thought she mumbled, "Morgan."

I remembered "Morgan" in German means "morning." Sighing, I said, "I guess we will have to stay here and take the train to Oradea in the morning."

Sleeping in the train station didn't seem like a good option. A train to Oradea the next morning didn't make sense to me either. I knew Oradea was just inside the Romanian border.

My ability to cope with the unexpected was being challenged. Suddenly, I felt God's calming hand, and I realized this had to be the Oradea station.

My ability to cope with the unexpected was being challenged.

My body ached after sixteen hours of travel. Our outdated Romanian travel book listed the Dacia Hotel as the best place to stay. Fred and I made our way down the crumbling concrete steps of the station, stepping around large puddles. Once outside the station, we easily found a taxi. As the driver loaded our bags into the trunk, two young Romanian men approached us.

"Are you Americans?" they asked.

We ignored them because in Vienna Duane had warned us about unscrupulous money changers on the streets preying upon innocent foreigners.

Again, they inquired, "Are you Americans?"

Again, we ignored them and continued to put our luggage in the trunk.

"Are you Karleen and Fred?"

I almost dropped to the ground as if I had seen two heavenly angels. How did they know our names?

How did they know our names?

Dan and Cornelius introduced themselves. I was amazed that we would be met by two men who knew our names.

"How did you know us, and how did you know which train we would be on?" I asked.

"Recently a pastor from Colorado visited Oradea. He urged us to meet you tonight. Sam Smith said when he arrived late and in the dark, he was frightened," Dan explained.

We met with Sam only once before we left home. We shared our mutual interest in Romania and some tentative travel plans. Later in Oradea, Sam told Dan and Cornelius we would be on this train. But how did Sam know? Originally, we planned to take an earlier train.

I explained to Dan and Cornelius our immediate crisis. "We lost our bag somewhere in the station in Budapest or on the train. Can you help us find it?"

Dan smiled. "This is Romania. You will never find that bag."

We had no choice but to believe him and to see our loss as a hopeless situation. I must have looked forlorn and disheartened.

"Don't worry. We will take care of you," Dan assured me.

"You can sleep in my house tonight," Cornelius said.

We got in their car and wound around the wet, dark, and narrow streets of Oradea until we came to Cornelius' house. I breathed a sigh of relief. Exhausted from our ordeal, we crawled into bed between beautifully hand embroidered, crisp white sheets . . . a far cry from sleeping in the train station as I had feared.

For the moment I felt safe.

The Hungarian countryside
looked like blobs of muted green and brown
on an artist's pallet.

3

The Power of Persecution

The life of persecuted Christians as a whole becomes the Fifth Gospel, an open, living, and walking testimony to the world, because those who are persecuted do not shame to present Christ to the world. Their lives yield fruits for the body of Christ. They become the occasion of bringing people to Christ.

Sheraz Khurram Khan, Pakistan
ASSIST News Service, February 1, 2007

After four long days of travel and jet lag, I slept from sheer exhaustion and awoke to the sound of a baby crying. As I looked around, I realized that we were sleeping in someone's living room. The night before, I was too tired to notice anything except an inviting bed. I stumbled out of bed trying to remember where Cornelius told us the bathroom was located. It was in a tiny space off the kitchen. While I was wandering around the kitchen in my bathrobe, Cornelius' wife, Valerie, came in and introduced herself. She had a two-month-old baby boy in her arms.

I asked if I could help her with the baby while she cooked some eggs for breakfast. Thinking we would be staying with Cornelius and Valerie for the week, I said, "I can help you with the baby this week just like a grandma." Valerie gave me a tentative smile which made me wonder if we were welcome for the week.

Cornelius sat down at the breakfast table and passionately told us his firsthand account of the revolution which took place less than two years before.

"The holidays were approaching, and Valerie and I were in Timisoara. Since we saw no hope for our future in Romania, we decided we would sneak across the border at night into Hungary.

"We were in a crowd that was peacefully demonstrating in front of a church. It was near the town center. Thousands of people were there holding candles and singing softly. They were tired of the repressive communist regime of the dictator, Nicolae Ceausescu. This was a revolution by 'candlelight.'

"Suddenly, we heard shots. The military had gathered and were firing at the crowd from across the town square. I pushed Valerie down on the ground, and we huddled there together. People who had been standing next to us were lying on the ground bleeding. Many were killed. I had my camera with me and took some pictures. Later, I was able to smuggle these out to some western journalists. It was a horrible time. We decided it was not safe to try to escape, and we went back home to Oradea."

This young Christian couple sitting before us had endured so much.

We sat stunned. This young Christian couple sitting before us had endured so much. Their greatest desire was to be free to worship without fear of reprisals. They simply longed for a better life. Since the revolution, they were full of hope and planned to go to the United States so that Cornelius could gain theological training and become a pastor in Romania. I thought, *We take such dreams for granted in the US.*

Even though we could have talked to Cornelius and Valerie all day, we needed to get dressed for church.

"Should I wear my head scarf?" I asked Cornelius.

"No. Visitors are not expected to conform to our traditions."

Now I wasn't sure what to do. "Well, what would the older ladies like?" I asked.

"Oh, they would love it if you wore a scarf."

Since I wanted to please all the ladies and not offend anyone, I donned my head scarf. I was thankful that before leaving Denver I had talked to folks who had been in Romanian churches.

At 10:30 in the morning Dan picked us up and took us to the Second Baptist Church of Oradea, now called Emanuel Baptist. He thought one of the pastors might possibly help us to connect with someone who worked with orphans.

On this Sunday there were crowds of people milling around the outside of an ordinary looking one-story building. The first service was over, and churchgoers were going into the building for the second service. The church had four services on Sunday, each with standing room only. Latecomers stood at the back and around the sides of the sanctuary.

As soon as we were inside the church building, Dan took my arm and guided me to where a group of ladies were sitting. Surprised, I thought, *What is he doing? I want to sit with Fred.* Then it dawned on me that women and men were not sitting together. This did not bode well with me, but soon the choir started to sing from the choir loft in the balcony. Their beautiful voices brought tears to my eyes. Here we were, finally, in Romania.

The church had four services on Sunday, each with standing room only.

The time in church went fast even though I could not understand a word spoken. I thought of all the persecution this church suffered during Nicolae Ceausescu's reign. He abhorred the Christian churches in Romania and tried to destroy them. Bible studies were forbidden and Ceausescu's spies scrutinized all church gatherings. I knew that the senior pastor, Joseph Tson, lived for years in Wheaton, Illinois, after being exiled from Romania for preaching the Gospel. During his exile, Pastor Tson founded the Romanian Missionary Society which provided invaluable support for Christians in Romania. Now Pastor Tson was back in the pulpit in Romania proclaiming the love of a mighty God who sustains us through all adversity.

Years before, I read *Tortured for Christ*, the story of Richard Wurmbrand, a pastor who suffered in a Romanian prison. The story of his dozen or so years in prison were etched in my memory. Wurmbrand used his years in prison to share the Gospel with his fellow inmates. He is quoted as saying, "To have spent many years in prison is not a disaster, but it is a disaster to have stayed long years in prison and have learned nothing from it. I have learned to love God very much, even when I suffer, and to love all people."

No matter what the communists did to squash Christianity in Romania, people of faith were multiplying by the thousands.

No matter what the communists did to squash Christianity in Romania, people of faith were multiplying by the thousands. Christians were determined to meet together in underground Bible studies and to continue their worship services. Under communism, hundreds of pastors and priests were sentenced to prison terms in one of Romania's five hundred prisons. Local congregations cared for the pastors' wives and children. The Christians who were sentenced to hard labor often had to slog through muck and mud building a worthless canal in Romania's Danube River delta. Yet this did not stop believers from proclaiming that Jesus Christ came to "set the prisoner free" and "save the people from their sins."

After the service, we were introduced to an older, retired couple. We were surprised when Dan said we would be staying with them for the week. The thought of staying the week with Cornelius and his wife had relieved my anxiety over the language barrier because they both spoke English. But it was not to be. Oh, I felt so disappointed. How would we ever communicate with someone who did not speak English?

Cornelius took us to Florica and Florio Monenciu's humble house. Chickens scurried around the courtyard. A fierce-looking dog threatened to break his chain as he lunged toward us. We were shown our room, the living room, with a couch that made into a bed. The living room also served as our dining room when the table was opened. I thought their multipurpose room was very clever.

Before leaving us with Florio and Florica, Cornelius surprised us with an invitation. "The pastors of the church invited you to meet them for prayer before the evening service. Dan will pick you up."

We were quite surprised at the invitation because we had only briefly met with one pastor after the morning service.

Florio
Fred
&
Florica

Florica and Florio smiled and laughed a lot which went far in helping us to feel at home. They fed us noodle soup, chicken and potatoes, and a delicious salad of bright red tomatoes and sliced cucumbers. No butter or margarine was served, so the bread tasted dry. The mineral water reminded me of Alka-Seltzer. During the meal, Florio stood at my right side encouraging me to eat more and more. I longed to tell him, *This is enough. I am very full.* At his urging, I accepted a small cup of black coffee after dinner. I am not a coffee drinker, and the strong brew shocked my taste buds.

Graciously, Florio and Florica rolled out the couch and motioned for us to have a rest. With the food removed and the door shut, the experience of all the different sights, sounds, and tastes suddenly overwhelmed me. I just wanted to close my eyes and block it all out for a few hours.

In order to sleep, I quickly discovered that I must either lie on the hump or the crack in the middle of the bed. Neither felt good. Finally, I found comfort on the edge of the bed by leaning against the wall. In the background, I could hear a rooster crowing and a dog barking. Only the living room wall separated me from the traffic noise on the street. Feeling very tired, I drifted off to sleep.

At five o'clock, Dan came to take us to the church. Upon entering a large conference room, we were greeted by the pastors and other visitors. Some were American missionaries who the pastors obviously knew. After introductions, Pastor Vidu asked Fred to pray for the evening service. We both thought this was a bit unusual because we were the newcomers. Fred prayed, and we moved into the sanctuary for the service.

> ### *During the years under the communist regime, churches were infiltrated with informers. Newcomers could not be trusted.*

Later, we realized this prayer was a test. Should they simply accept that we were truly believers in Jesus Christ? During the years under the communist regime, churches were infiltrated with informers. Newcomers could not be trusted. Naively, we thought we would immediately be accepted since we were Christians from America.

We found our seats in the sanctuary, and the service began. During the service, when we heard our names spoken, we thought the pastor was introducing visitors to the congregation. Afterwards, Dan looked at me and said, "Pastor Vidu announced that you would be teaching a seminar Monday evening. I will be your translator."

Wow! I didn't expect this. A nervous chill ran down my spine. But after all, wasn't this why I came?

I was moved by the extreme poverty—especially in the rural Gypsy villages where there is no running water, no windows, and no doors on the buildings. We also visited an apartment building for Gypsies where they kept their horses and livestock inside the rooms so they would not be stolen.

James

4

Facing Prejudice

Bury me standing, I've been on my knees all my life.
A Gypsy Saying

Sunday evening after church, Dan suggested we go and meet a doctor from Sweden who knew about the orphans. As we opened the door to her apartment, quite a sight greeted us. Clotheslines laden with wet crib sheets and diapers filled the rooms. The only space without a clothesline was above her bed.

I don't know what I expected from a Swedish doctor, but Inger Bostrom amazed me. She was warm and outgoing with a glow in her green eyes, a big smile, and an even bigger heart. All the sheets and diapers were from Marghita Hospital.

Every day, Inger drove an hour north to the small town of Marghita to visit abandoned babies in the pediatric section of Marghita Hospital. Each day when Inger left the hospital, she brought home the soiled sheets and diapers to wash them. Her apartment was equipped with a washing machine, but she did not have a dryer.

Was I impressed! Inger truly wanted to do whatever needed to be done to help the children.

As we sat on Inger's bed, she told us about orphans and Romanian culture. She assured us that Romanian women truly love their children, but over 80 percent of abandoned children are Gypsy, and Romanians look down on the Gypsies.

"But why?" I asked.

"Gypsies are very poor and cannot afford to care for their large families. Most of the Gypsy women are married when they are in their early teens. A young woman may have as many as five or six children by the time she is twenty. It is common for a Gypsy mother, exhausted after delivery, to quietly walk away and leave her baby in the hospital.

Years later, when the children are in an orphanage, their parents may come back for them so they can either beg or work in the fields."

I shook my head. I couldn't grasp the concept of a mother giving up her baby. I bowed my head whispering, "Oh, dear God." I wondered what went on in a woman's heart to take this step. The problem must be more than material poverty, but instead, a "poverty" in a mother's heart.

> ## *I couldn't grasp the concept of a mother giving up her baby.*

Inger continued. "Most Romanian women find it very difficult to care for the abandoned Gypsy children. Gypsy orphans are not accepted in Romanian society. The Gypsies have dark skin and are considered thieves. Many Romanian families are too poor to take in an orphan, and they might be afraid of the orphan's family. Few Romanians understand the life abandoned children experience in an orphanage."

Inger and I shared our concerns for the early development of an abandoned infant. We both understood that a baby who does not experience love and nurture suffers pervasive developmental delays.

I knew that during the communist years, western information about child development was not allowed into Romania. Few people in Romania understood how institutionalized care would impact a child, and most had never been inside an orphanage or the hospitals where abandoned babies lived for the first two to three years of their lives. They just assumed the children were receiving good care.

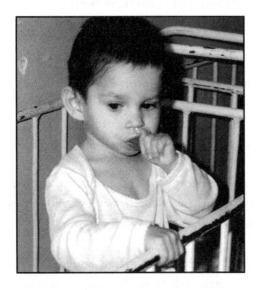

A baby who does not experience love and nurture suffers pervasive developmental delays.

"So the conditions really are as bad as I saw on that 20/20 program?" I asked.
"Come. Come with me tomorrow and see," Inger said.

Who are the Gypsies?

Years before going to Romania, I developed a fascination with the Gypsy people. I read about the poor and rich Gypsies all over the world. Even though they have never had a homeland to call their own, their history drifts in and out of the shadows of world history.

The most prevalent question is where did the Gypsies come from? The Roma, as they are also called in Romania, originally migrated from India. They traveled to Turkey and soon fled from forced Islamic conversions by the Turks. The Gypsy world is as old as the fourteenth century, when the ancestors of what now are an estimated eight million Gypsies started to arrive from India. They scattered all over Europe especially in what are now former communist countries. Their transient lifestyle and clannishness keep them out of the mainstream of society. Gypsies travel either by walking or by Conestoga-style horse drawn wagon. Many Gypsies live in their own villages separate from Romanians.

According to the 1991 Helsinki Watch report, "Gypsies were persecuted in Transylvania (then under Hungarian rule, but now under Romanian) where they were forced into slave labor by the Crown. By the mid-nineteenth century, many rose up to oppose slavery and it was abolished in 1855." During World War II, Gypsies were considered criminals and were to be eliminated. The severest discrimination was meted out by the Nazis during the Holocaust. They faced the same fate as the Jewish populations and were deported to concentration camps where they perished.

During World War II,
Gypsies were considered criminals
and were to be eliminated.
Gypsies continue to experience harassment
all over Eastern Europe.

Gypsies continue to experience harassment all over Eastern Europe. Why are these folks so feared and disrespected? I have sensed that it's because there is aura of mystery that surrounds them. They do keep to themselves and their own ways, which may be contrary to the norms of the Romanian community. They marry their daughters off at a very early age, and children are cared for in "communal" style.

Gypsies in Romania have been the target of violent attacks since the revolution that toppled Nicolae Ceausescu. Their homes have been burned, and they have been beaten and chased out of villages. (See *Destroying Ethnic Identity, The Persecution of Gypsies in Romania*, Helsinki Watch Report, a division of Human Rights Watch, September, 1991.)

Gypsies experience discrimination in most areas of life. They frequently have the worst housing, and their children are not welcome in school or are seated in the back of the classroom. Because they are Gypsy children they are considered "slow," and it is assumed that they will misbehave.

Gypsies, with their dark skin, are the most visible ethnic minority and are easily targeted.

Gypsies, with their dark skin, are the most visible ethnic minority and are easily targeted. They make up about 10 percent of Romania's population. The name "Gypsy" is considered derogatory and most would rather be called Roma or Romanies.

My own experience with the Gypsies of Romania is varied. One night I was invited to a Gypsy church. I was asked to share with the group why I am in Romania. As I spoke about the children abandoned by their mothers, I noticed several of the women crying. *Were they crying because they had abandoned a child they loved and they were too poor to take the child back?*

It was a cold night and we were all bundled up, but I could see the women's colorful gathered skirts and head scarves. The small room was poorly lit and the wood stove smoked. I asked if something was wrong with the stove. The answer was, "No, it is always like this." They did have windows in their humble building which I learned was not always the case.

I saw Gypsy women carrying babies in Oradea. They were usually begging, but often would have flowers or mushrooms to sell. The women look very old and wrinkled. Their faces give testimony to their hard life. Most of the older women I saw were missing teeth. Unless you have money to have your teeth cared for, they are just pulled leaving gaps. I was told that a woman who looks in her 60s or 70s might only be in her 40s.

Unless you have money to have your teeth cared for, they are just pulled leaving gaps.

One day in Oradea, I saw a boy and his mother walking up to cars selling flowers. A police car drove up and grabbed the boy. They shoved him in the trunk of the car and slammed the lid. I could not believe my eyes. The mother was distraught as the police car drove away down the street. I was horrified. *What were the police planning to do with the boy? Would they detain him for a day or two and then free him? Would they take him to an orphanage? If so, how would this apparently penniless mother find him?* To me, this was the perfect example of a woman and child who were helpless and had no legal rights.

At any one time, 10 percent of the Gypsies in Romania travel throughout the countryside and camp out alongside of the road. Around the wagons I noticed blankets and cookware spread on the ground. The next morning everything was packed up and they were gone.

The Romanian government has attempted to encourage the Gypsies to settle in one area. The government has built small houses for them on the edge of a town or village. Usually, this location is not the most desirable, but it is a place to live. One such location has a dozen houses all painted a bright green. They look a little out of place with the more earth-toned village houses.

There are a disproportionate number of dark skinned children in orphanages. I believe that poverty, the high birth rate, and economic oppression afflict many of the Gypsy families and cause them to give up their children. When a high rate of alcoholism is added, it is apparent that it would be a struggle to bring up children in a good, safe environment. Sadly, the women and the children are the disenfranchised ones.

I wonder why I was born.
My life was over before it began,
because my mother did not care about me.
No one loves a Gypsy.
We have no future; no one will hire us.
They hate us because we steal.

Orphan teen

Gypsy mom
& child
at
Marghita
Hospital

5

Turn My Eyes Away

***Turn my eyes away from what
my heart cannot bear to see.***

’ll never forget our first ride with Inger to Marghita Hospital early that Monday morning. Marghita is an hour's drive from Oradea . . . if you drive the speed limit.

As Inger whizzed down the road, she asked Fred, sitting in the front seat, if her speeding bothered him.

He said, "No. I pray a lot." We laughed and held on as we sped through villages and over slick cobblestone streets.

As she drove, Inger picked up our conversation from the previous evening. "The orphanages are usually in small villages in the countryside. High concrete walls prevent the village people from seeing the disturbed and emaciated children inside."

"That reminds me of a story I heard of a pastor in Timisoara," I said. [Timisoara is a large city several hours south of Oradea near the Hungarian border.]

"When speaking to an aid worker from Scotland, this pastor said, 'I doubt that there are as many orphans in Romania as the western journalists have reported.' In fact, he boasted that there were no orphanages in Timisoara. To prove his point, he went around the city looking for such places. He returned a very humbled man because he found an orphanage just two blocks from his church. Nobody knew what was behind those walls until he checked with the gatekeeper. The pastor was shocked at what he found and asked the aid worker to assist his church in helping the children."

Inger told me that often hundreds of children are sequestered in an orphanage and not allowed to go outside to play like normal children. They are kept in their beds most of the time.

How do they keep these children in bed all day? I asked myself. Are they too weak to play or make noise? Could they have been drugged? It was unbelievable to even consider either of these possibilities.

Finally, we arrived in Marghita, a town which reminded me of how our western towns in the US used to look. The wind blew dust twisters in the main street. Now and then a hungry looking dog wandered into the street. We drove through the hospital gate, innocents about to be initiated into the world of Romanian orphans.

How do they keep these children in bed all day?

Marghita Hospital, under the Ministry of Health, took responsibility for abandoned children until their mothers came back for them or until the children turned three. Then the children were moved to an orphanage. Children with the slightest handicap, such as crossed eyes, were sent to an institution for so-called "irrecoupables." These children had no hope of ever living a normal life outside an institution.

Fred, Inger, and I walked through the grassy courtyard where green benches were scattered about. Peeling paint from the benches exposed rusting iron. Hospital patients in gray bathrobes lounged here and there.

High concrete walls surrounded the hospital compound. Various medical problems were treated in different buildings of the hospital. The pediatric section, located in a three-story building, was for newborns, sick children, and abandoned babies. Offices and treatment rooms were on the first floor, maternity on the second floor, and rooms for abandoned babies and toddlers on the third floor.

A strong medicinal odor greeted us as we entered the building. We climbed the well-worn concrete stairs to the third floor. Rays of sunlight filtered through windows high above the stairs and splashed onto the dark walls. A nurse in a white coat opened a door and entered the hallway. She quickly disappeared into another room, closing the door behind her.

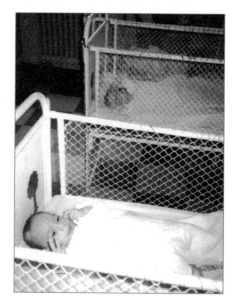

Six very pale babies lay in metal cribs with chain-link sides.

Upon reaching the third floor, the pattern of small alternating brown and gray vinyl floor tiles caught my eye. In the corridor, the white, wooden doors to the babies' rooms were closed. Inger said only three rooms were open to us. Cautiously, we entered the first room. We were greeted with total silence. Six very pale babies lay in metal cribs with chain link sides. Their small bodies were cradled in urine-soaked, horsehair mattresses punctured by broken metal springs.

Tightly swaddled in rags, the babies barely moved. One tiny baby girl had brown hair with a widow's peak framing her sweet little face. Her chin tilted up revealing a dimple in the center. Long, black eyelashes made her dark eyes seem enormous. In contrast, her pale skin reminded me of a porcelain doll. This precious baby girl's eyes connected with mine. I tried to persuade her to smile with cheerful sounding words. Her small size suggested a baby only a few months old, but a mouthful of teeth told me she was much older. Her thin arms moved slightly. In her weak condition, the indentation her body made in the mattress limited her movement. Day upon day staring up from her crib, she saw only a blank ceiling.

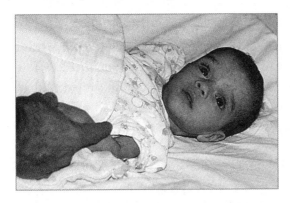

Tightly swaddled in rags, the babies barely moved.

I couldn't believe a child could be allowed to waste away like this. As I picked her up, tears came to my eyes. Her feathery light body felt stiff as a board. Quietly I asked, "Oh, God, what is wrong with this child?" Our eyes connected and hers locked with mine. I wondered if my heart could bear the pain of knowing this young girl's story.

I could hear a wheeze from his chest. Paper-thin skin hung from his bones. His big eyes and gaunt look was one I have only seen in pictures of Holocaust prisoners. He definitely was physically challenged, possibly with cerebral palsy. I guessed his age as three. Someone had dressed him in a nice knit striped shirt, but his big, bulky diapers were made of rags. When Fred lifted Petrica, he stiffened as if this was a new experience for

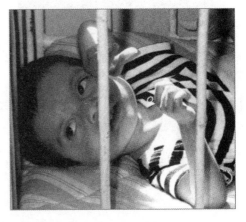

him. Fred spoke softly to him, and he began to focus his eyes on Fred's face. I could see his body relax, and soon we saw a little smile creep across his face. Who knows how much more Petrica could have enjoyed life if there was someone to take him out of his crib during the day.

"What will happen to him this winter?" I asked Inger.

"If he gets pneumonia, he probably will not survive. The winters are very cold here, and these huge buildings with high ceilings are hard to heat. If the children get no fresh air and not enough proper nutrition, their immune system is compromised. Poor Petrica. This little boy will surely catch influenza. It is hopeless. There is nothing we can do. It is hopeless."

Was he just a throwaway child no one wanted to be bothered with?

A feeling of overpowering sadness welled up inside me at the eventuality that Petrica might not survive the winter. Was he just a throwaway child no one wanted to be bothered with? Did the medical staff see his fate as inevitable and decide not to care? With all the suffering and repulsive odors around me, I thought for a moment that I was going to pass out. *Surely this must be a dream. I am not really seeing this, am I?* I knew from this moment on I would never be the same. I turned and walked out of Petrica's room. My heart could not bear anymore.

Inger arranged for us to take the children outside in the courtyard for some fresh air. She laid blankets down for the little ones and set up an infant swing. We carried the children outside. Petrica's smile grew a little wider as Fred laid him on one of the blankets. We sat on the ground next to him and the other babies, basking in the moments of freedom we could give them.

After an hour, we carried the babies back to the third floor. It was frustrating to change their diapers as we had only cold water and no toilet facilities. The diapers were placed in a pile in a small closet.

Fred, Inger, and I continued to hold the babies one by one until it was time to go. We whispered words of love to them and sang softly, "Jesus loves me this I know . . ." into his ears. What else could we do with such helpless feelings.

I longed to shout, "Doesn't anyone here care about these babies?" Somehow, I sensed the answer would be only silence . . . except for the woeful cooing sounds of the "mourning doves" drifting through the windows.

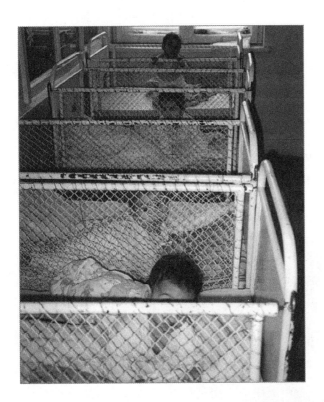

I could NOT
"turn my eyes away"

as God called me
to "see," really "see"
these babies the
way He sees them.

They are infinitely
more precious than
gold or diamonds.

They are the children
who Jesus invites
to come to Him.

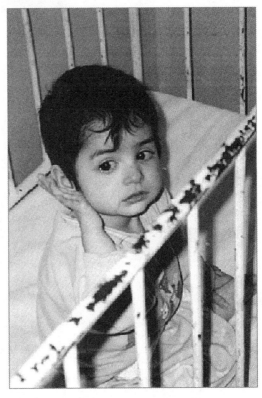

I wanted to weep for hours and hours
after what I had just experienced.

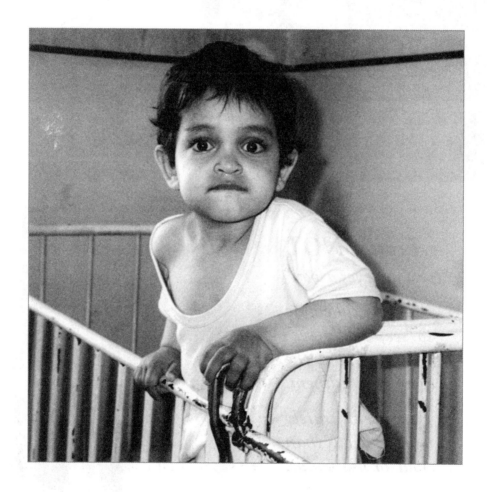

6

Signs and Wonders

I will give thanks to the LORD with all my heart;
I will tell of all Thy wonders.

Psalm 9:1 NASB

Inger, Fred, and I rode back to Oradea after visiting the abandoned babies in Marghita Hospital. There was no lighthearted chitchat. I felt like the evil of this world had been fleshed out for me at the sight of these helpless babies. My body was limp and my heart aching. I wanted to weep for hours and hours at what I had just experienced. Emotionally I felt that I had no more to give to Romania that day. The last thing I desired to do was to stand before a group of people that evening and speak to them on caring for the orphans. It was difficult to think about the suffering babies without weeping.

We arrived at Florio and Florica's around four in the afternoon. I could see the concern in their eyes when they looked at me. I longed to communicate with them and tell them what we just witnessed. I knew it was typical that most Romanians did not even know such children existed.

Mentally I tried to prepare for my first seminar in Romania, but I found it difficult to focus. I couldn't forget the stiffness of the babies I held or their fragility. I was still in shock after seeing crib after crib of babies who did not smile and whose little hands tried to grasp my fingers. My tears were on the brink of letting go. With a deep breath, I gathered up my visuals and notes on *Mothering the Unmothered* and left for church.

Speaking to Romanian women interested in caring for orphans gave me confidence that we could be of use in Romania.

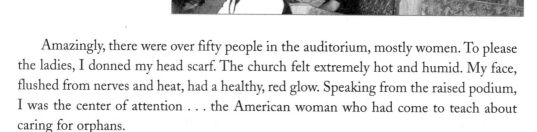

Amazingly, there were over fifty people in the auditorium, mostly women. To please the ladies, I donned my head scarf. The church felt extremely hot and humid. My face, flushed from nerves and heat, had a healthy, red glow. Speaking from the raised podium, I was the center of attention . . . the American woman who had come to teach about caring for orphans.

I asked Fred to read some Scripture so all would know I spoke under the authority of my husband. I didn't know how the people would view a woman teaching in the sanctuary.

As I began to speak, a lightheaded feeling rushed over me. I kept saying to myself, *This is why I came. Lord, help me get through this.* I tried not to use American slang; I didn't know how to pace my words. Pausing for the translation gave me a chance to glance at my notes from time to time. Even though I am sure I made mistakes, I received many hugs, kisses on both cheeks, and "thank-yous" after the lecture. Speaking to Romanian women interested in caring for orphans gave me confidence that we could be of use in Romania.

Little did I know that Inger had brought her Swedish friend, Barbro Gustavsson, to hear me speak or that God would give us a friendship and partnership in ministering to orphans that now spans almost two decades.

All of this happened in my first two days in Romania.

The events of the third day were encouraging. Dan showed us around Oradea and introduced us to two Christian doctors who were opening Bethany Christian Clinic, a private clinic in a Hungarian Baptist church building.

Private clinics were not allowed prior to 1989 under the communist regime. Now the new government allowed medical professionals the freedom to set up their own practice and clinics.

Dr. Benjamin Pardi and Dr. Moise Mateas had just begun to unpack the supplies for their clinic. Boxes of donated pharmaceuticals and crates of medical instruments filled the several rooms set aside for the clinic.

Doctors Pardi and Mateas greeted us cordially. Both appeared to be in their thirties. Dr. Mateas was tall and lanky. Dr. Pardi's smile gave me the feeling that he was a man who had an inner joy. Both doctors were excited to be starting up a clinic in their hometown of Oradea. They enthusiastically showed us several donated medical instruments and asked if we could help them find a part for an ultrasound machine. "Some companies in the West donate medical equipment with broken parts," Dr. Pardi explained.

"Are these parts available in Romania?" Fred asked.

"Impossible," Dr. Mateas said.

"Romania does not have modern equipment like this. We need this ultrasound to use with pregnant women and their babies, but it doesn't work. There is only one other ultrasound in this country and it is in Bucharest," Dr. Pardi said.

We assured the doctors we would try to find the part in the US and get it to them. They were excited. Switching on his small flashlight, Fred looked for the name of the company and a serial number on the back of the machine. He was astonished. The instrument was made in the US in Denver, our home town. Amazing! Another sign that we could help in Romania.

Our next stop was a site a few kilometers outside Oradea where Swedish and American visionaries, Lars and Linda Hornberg, planned to build a Christian orphanage called Caminul Felix. Lars formerly pastored a church in Sweden. As a single American woman, Linda performed as a soloist for many years in Romania before the fall of communism. Even with no children of their own, Linda and Lars loved children and especially the orphans. Their plan for Caminul Felix was to have ten to twelve orphans live in each of six cottages with houseparents to look after them. The children would remain with the houseparents until they were old enough to be on their own. I was sorry that the Hornbergs were out of the country as I felt we were kindred spirits. After we returned home, Lars sent us a letter inviting us teach the orphanage staff the following summer.

Our place of rest and home base during our first week was Florio and Florica's home. These two dear, simple, and loving folks quickly stole our hearts. On our third evening at their house, Florica wanted to sing some hymns. We went outside into their grassless courtyard and sat on a wooden bench. Florica started to sing "Amazing Grace" in Romanian. We wanted to sing with her, but hearing the familiar hymn sung in Romanian, we simply could not bring forth the English words. Across the courtyard wall, Florio and Florica's neighbor raised his head above the wall and started to sing with us.

Here we were surrounded by clucking hens and singing "Amazing Grace" with three Romanians.

As the sun began to set, the sky turned brilliant orange. All around, stucco houses with red tile roofs glowed in the fading light. Sitting in a tree silhouetted against the sky, the neighbor reminded me of the fiddler in the film *Fiddler on the Roof*. Here we were surrounded by clucking hens and singing "Amazing Grace" with three Romanians. Was I dreaming or really here? For a moment, I did not know. My heart filled with gratitude that God had taken us safely this far.

Early on our fourth day in Romania, we were awakened to pounding on the living room door. Florica shouted, "Karleen si Fred, repede, repede, telefon!" Puzzled over the uproar, we looked at each other. Fred hurried to the phone and spoke for a few moments. He came back and said, "You will never guess what has happened."

Fred recounted the story Dan had told him over the phone. With tears running down his cheeks, he smiled and said, "Our zipper bag has been found!"

"Our zipper bag has been found!"

When boarding the train in Budapest, a Romanian man saw our black zipper bag on the train platform. As we were hurrying off the train, he boarded another car with our bag. In the bag, the man found a paper with a name and phone number of a Romanian woman. Later, after arriving home in his village in the Transylvanian mountains, he called the number. Speaking with Dr. Rodica Urziceanu, he said he was looking for the "master of this bag." Rodica, who had visited us in Denver earlier in the year, had written down her name and phone number just in case we went to Bucharest. Rodica called Tim Bale, an American missionary in Bucharest. Before we left home, we had faxed Tim the only contact number we had in Oradea, that of Lars Hornberg. Dan was staying at the Hornbergs' house while they were in Sweden. He received Rodica's call and said he would get in touch with us right away.

We were awed by this complicated chain of events. But that wasn't all.

"The man agreed to take the twelve hour overnight train ride to Oradea to return the bag to us," Fred said. Joy erupted. It was a miracle. God was with us and cared about our every need.

We threw on our clothes and went with Dan to the train station. I asked Fred, "How will we know this man?"

"He will have our bag!" Fred laughed.

"This doesn't happen in Romania," Dan said.
"This is a miracle."

As we pulled into the station parking lot, we saw a tall, gaunt-looking man holding our bag. When I walked up to him, he did the most beautiful thing. He took my hand and kissed it as a true Romanian gentleman would. I gasped and said, "Oh, I should be kissing your hand." Of course, he did not speak English, but he must have seen how delighted we were to have our bag returned. Although he asked nothing in return, we insisted on reimbursing him for his train fare and the wages he lost coming to Oradea.

Both Dan and Cornelius shook their heads.

"This doesn't happen in Romania," Dan said. "This is a miracle."

We bowed our heads and thanked God.

I wondered,

What else does God have in store for us?

In this personal odyssey
  of catastrophic events,
there is this rising, absorbing thought:
  God knows and feels our pain.
Just as my Lord did at the grave of Lazarus,
He weeps with me.
My God weeps.

James Means
A Tearful Celebration
Finding God in the Midst of Loss

7

A Difficult Parting

The LORD's lovingkindnesses indeed never cease.
For His compassions never fail.
They are new every morning;
Great is Your faithfulness.
Lamentations 3:22–23 NASB

Hmmm," the doctor said as he looked at the X-ray of my foot. "It's not broken. However, it is badly bruised. Some of the blood vessels are ruptured. You should stay off it for at least three days."

"But I am supposed to leave for Romania tomorrow morning. Should I still go?" I asked.

"Your foot should be okay in a few days. Meanwhile, ask for a wheelchair in the airport."

Oh, great, I thought. *I am leaving on my second missions trip to Romania in a wheelchair.*

Several months after our first trip into Romania in 1991, we began preparing to take a team with us the following summer. The folks who offered to go were all professionals involved in some area of pediatrics. Our team consisted of our family doctor, a neonatal nurse, a special education teacher, an occupational therapist, a speech pathologist, and a musician. Fred was the team leader and experienced father of adopted and foster children. I was the specialist in early childhood development. Collectively, we had a lot of knowledge and experience to offer the staff of Romanian orphanages. With a better understanding of the needs of abandoned children, the staff could raise the level of care in the orphanages, and the lives of the orphans would improve. Or so I thought.

During the winter and spring, our Loving Arms team, as we called ourselves, met once a month. Fred and I shared experiences of our first trip in 1991. We explained what we knew of life in Romania.

The country had been free from communism only a little over two years. Free enterprise had not yet taken hold. Most of the stores were empty or carried a limited supply of groceries and goods, a far cry from what we have in the States. The team would have to survive without juice, pop, pizza, hamburgers, and drinkable running water. Breakfast would consist of goat cheese, salami, and tomatoes washed down with strong coffee. We might or might not have a comfortable bed or hot water for showers. We would have to be flexible at every turn. Everyone on the team agreed in principle, but we did not realize what "tests" lay ahead for us.

We did not realize what "tests" lay ahead for us.

In the spring, Lars and Linda Hornberg's orphanage, Caminul Felix, opened on the outskirts of Oradea and was filling up fast. Lars' assistant from Colorado, Debbie Steffens, was a young and enthusiastic recent graduate of Wheaton College in Illinois. We met Debbie in Denver before our first trip in 1991. Debbie's ponytail bounced as she talked. Her smile radiated as she spoke of her love for the orphans. Debbie amazed us with her fluency in speaking the Romanian language.

In May, Debbie faxed our team. "I have invited staff from all the orphanages in the Bihor (county) area. I don't know how many will come, but I have rented a large conference hall at the nearby resort of Baile Felix. We are planning a three-day conference presented by the Loving Arms team."

Once our friends in Romania knew we were coming in July, we received several more invitations to teach. Dr. Rodica Urziceanu invited us to the university in Bucharest where her clinic for autistic children was located. She invited professionals including many orphanage directors in Bucharest. In Marghita, Inger spoke to a pastor's wife, Luci Cocis, about our Loving Arms team. Luci invited us to speak to the ladies of her church and staff from orphanages in the area. She also extended an invitation to a Marghita Hospital pediatrician, Dr. Katrina Lupau.

Our last invitation came from a Romanian woman who escaped communist Romania by swimming across the Danube River. She made her way to the US and later graduated from Denver Seminary. She returned to Romania to start a Bible school in the southern city of Drobeta Turnu Severin on the Danube. Our team was asked to come to teach and encourage the students.

When we weren't teaching or traveling, we planned to spend time visiting orphans. While the Loving Arms team was driving throughout Romania, Dr. David Miller, our team doctor, would work alongside Drs. Pardi and Mateas at Bethany Christian Clinic in Oradea. Our plans were coming together. The Loving Arms team had an exciting but taxing schedule ahead.

However, here I was the night before our departure with an ice pack on my foot. To make matters worse, my mother was not well. She lived in an assisted living center forty-five minutes from our home. This evening was our last chance to visit with her before we left for Europe, but my throbbing foot was too painful for me to go anywhere. So Fred went to say our good-byes.

Mom was distressed when I did not come.

She told Fred, "I see Karleen in the hall. Why won't she come in and see me?"

"Mom, Karleen is not here. She hurt her foot and could not come tonight," Fred replied.

My heart ached when Fred told me about his visit. "Mom was too confused to understand why you couldn't come," he said.

"Maybe she will think I don't want to see her. We'll be home in three weeks, and I know the children will visit her." Even as I spoke those words, I was not really convinced Mom would be okay. Later, I would deeply regret my failure to visit Mom the night before our departure for Romania.

> *Later, I would deeply regret my failure*
> *to visit Mom the night before*
> *our departure for Romania.*

Fred and I and our daughters, Wendi and Christine, ages ten and eleven, planned a week-long vacation in Oxford, England, before our rendezvous with the Loving Arms team in Austria, south of Munich, Germany. The flight across the Atlantic was a long one. My foot became more painful as it began to swell. By the time, we arrived at Heathrow airport in London, I was thankful that we had asked for wheelchair assistance. We rented a car and drove to Oxford. The road signs were difficult for us to decipher, and driving on the left side of the road was a challenge for Fred.

The charming, old-world atmosphere of Oxford captivated us. We climbed the city tower to see the countless Oxford limestone steeples. It was a thrilling experience to sit in the chapel of the college where C. S. Lewis taught. I could imagine him walking down the cloister mingling with students and in deep theological discussions.

"Why do those students have on black robes?" Wendi asked.

"It is a tradition here for students and professors to wear black robes," I said. "Many things in England are based on very old traditions."

"It is so cool to be here," Wendi said.

I laughed, as indeed it was. As my foot began to feel better, we drove out to the countryside and hiked a short distance to a lovely Cotswold village. We delighted in eating fish and chips on the town green. I felt we needed this time to relax. The countless details involved in preparing to take a team to Romania had been stressful.

Our holiday mood changed abruptly when we returned in the late afternoon to our cottage just outside Oxford. There was a message from our son. "Call home immediately. Scott." We had left instructions with Scott regarding how he could reach us if there was an emergency with Grandma.

Since we had no phone in our cottage, we asked to use a neighbor's phone.

Scott spoke softly. "Mary, Ben, and I had a good visit with Grandma in the afternoon. The kids sat on her bed, and she smiled and talked to them. She seemed happy. A few hours later, the hospital called to say that Grandma died in her sleep."

It was strange, because although the day had been perfectly lovely, I had a foreboding in one corner of my heart. Something is not right. Something is wrong.

Now what should we do? We had five team members traveling to Austria to meet us. Fred and I were the only ones who had been to Romania. After talking with Scott, we decided that Mom would be buried, and we would have a graveside service for her after we returned home. The decision not to go home was one of the most difficult I have ever made in my life. It remains a puzzle to me why God took me to Europe where I could not be with her when she died. I did not even have a chance to say good-bye.

> *The decision not to go home*
> *was one of the most difficult*
> *I have ever made in my life.*

After an emotional few hours of phone calls with family members, Fred and I needed some time alone to absorb the shock of Mom's dying. We decided to take a walk down by the river. The English garden of our cottage, bordered by the River Thames, was a blend of ivy, gorgeous cobalt-blue delphiniums, red roses, lilies, and snapdragons. Fred and I stood arm in arm in this peaceful place. I cried softly. As we stood there, the sun sank in a fiery red ball beyond the river. The sun's reflection turned the river into gold silk-like ripples flowing past the flowered banks. I have never seen such an awesome sunset. I believe the beauty of those moments was God's gift of comfort to me.

With much sorrow in our hearts, we went on to meet the team as planned. In the days ahead, I would ask myself many times . . .

> *Am I up to leading this team*
> *into Romania*
> *and the many tasks that lie ahead?*

8

Heady and Heartbreaking Days

When thou passest through the waters, I will be with thee;
and through the rivers, they shall not overflow thee.

Isaiah 43:2 KJV

Our vacation in England was soon over and we needed to meet the team and go on with our mission to Romania. We all met in Mittersill, Austria, the location of a Christian conference center called Schloss Mittersill. This ancient castle with its stunning view of the Alps was a perfect place for us to recover from jet lag and bond together as a team. Because Mom had been Dr. Miller's patient for many years, he was the one person on the team who knew her. His gentle manner of inquiring about my loss soothed my aching heart. Though feeling low in my spirit I was determined to go on with our mission.

Our transportation to Romania proved to be complicated. No rental agency wanted to rent a van for travel to Romania, although they would rent cars. The team had no other choice than to rent three cars in Munich.

After a day's rest at Schloss Mittersill and a day of sightseeing in Vienna, we were more than eager to hit the road for Romania in our shiny, red cars. As we drove farther east through Hungary, the towns looked less and less affluent. We saw a McDonald's restaurant outside of Budapest and stopped for lunch. Hungarian is not an easy language, and it was difficult to order food, even at McDonald's. Finding a gas station was also a problem, but at last we saw one a short distance from the Romanian border. We had spent the last of our local currency on hamburgers, but the attendant took our dollars only to grossly overcharge us by giving us a very bad exchange rate. A "good news, bad news" experience.

Finally, we approached what appeared to be a mile-long line of cars and trucks. We thought they must be waiting to cross the border into Romania. The guards were having dinner and changing shifts so we sat for hours.

The Romanian embassy in the US told us visas were available at the border for $30 each, but this requirement could be waived for humanitarian workers. The Romanian border guards said the law had changed . . . just that very day. In the summer of 1992, every American had to pay $30 for a visa.

"What a waste of money," I whispered. "They charge us $300 for our team to come and help."

"We'll have to pay it in order to move on," Fred said. "It's getting dark and I think we should be on our way."

The guard motioned to Fred to open the trunk of our car. "Any electronic equipment?" he asked.

The guard motioned to Fred to open the trunk of our car.

Fred started to say no, but then the guard pointed to a box. "What's this?"

"It's an audiometer for testing hearing," Fred explained.

We had not thought of this out-of-date instrument as electronic equipment. How did this guard know to look in this particular box in our trunk crammed full of supplies?

"Take this equipment to the doctor in that building," he said, pointing to a one-story building next to the guard station. "You need to have a doctor's permission to bring this into Romania."

In the end, we paid for our visas and found a man who called himself a doctor. He scribbled his name and stamped the paper. We were waved on into Romania.

As we left the border, we saw that there were others who were unloading everything from their vehicles. We had heard tales of cigarettes and whiskey being passed to the guards to gain their favor, but we were not the bribing kind. It took us about four hours to get through the border.

We were not the bribing kind. It took us about four hours to get through the border.

Evading numerous potholes, we entered Oradea about fifteen minutes later. It was now dark, and the city had no streetlights. In the darkness, we could not recognize any landmarks that we had seen the year before. We were lost. At each intersection one of us had to get out of the car with a flashlight to read the street sign.

We were lost.

Finally, we stopped the car and I asked an old man, "Unde Hotel Poienita?" I have no idea what else he said, but I heard the word "trei." He must mean the third building down the street. My few words of Romanian paid off. We rejoiced when we arrived at the hotel. It looked like something right out of the communist era in a 50s movie . . . olive drab carpet and orange upholstered furniture. Our team settled into their rooms. It was too late to go to the hotel restaurant for dinner. We relied on the cheese, salami, and bread we brought with us from Austria.

The day after our arrival, we rested and worked on our teaching plans. The following morning we nervously walked from our hotel to the conference hall a couple of blocks away. Over two hundred people gathered to hear us speak about caring for abandoned children. The large audience shocked us. Would our seminar be practical to all these folks?

Fred stepped to the platform to welcome those in attendance. He introduced me as the first speaker. With some anxiety, I began my presentation of "Mothering the Unmothered." The audience was the largest I had ever spoken to. Early that morning, Fred had prayed with me in preparation for the seminar. I had spoken on this subject several times and knew the material well, but emotionally I struggled.

Over two hundred people gathered to hear us speak about caring for abandoned children.

After lunch, our speech pathologist took the podium. Then we opened a time for questions. Suddenly, what seemed like an angry debate broke out with several participants talking at the same time. With no understanding of the language, we did not know what the issues were. I thought, *Oh, no! What have we done?* Dan translated. The issue was a disagreement over using pacifiers with babies. The exchange was so intense I thought World War III might begin. But after this passionate debate, the group settled down and the day ended peacefully. The Romanians started to shake hands as if nothing had happened. There were smiles everywhere and hugs and kisses for the presenters.

I looked at Dan and asked, "What happened? They seemed so angry at each other one minute and very jovial the next."

"Don't worry," Dan said. "This is the way it is in our culture. Romanians can debate passionately about any subject, but we remain friends."

The second and third day went the same way. After the final presentation, we handed out Certificates of Completion to all the participants. They thanked us, and many of them hugged us and kissed us on both cheeks. A few stopped to ask some questions about their own children.

"My baby is just two months old. My mother says if I pick her up when she cries, I will spoil her. What should I do?" asked one young woman.

"Well, what does your mother's heart say?" I responded.

"Oh, that I should pick her up."

"Well, then go and do it. Explain to your mother that you believe when your baby cries you should pick her up and soothe her." I was rewarded with a sigh of relief and a glowing smile.

First Loving Arms Team - 1992

When the conference was over, we loaded our bags into our three cars and began the twelve hour drive to Bucharest. Navigating winding roads and dodging ever-present potholes were enough to make the strongest carsick. We were making good time until we came to a construction area. When we slowed down because of loose gravel . . . wham! Another car rear-ended us. As the drivers sized up the damage, the pretty, young daughter of the Romanian driver walked up to us.

"Are you Americans?" she asked in English.

"Yes, we are. We came to Romania to teach orphanage staff," I said.

"I can't believe this!" she exclaimed. "I am actually standing here talking to Americans."

"Where did you learn to speak such good English?" I asked.

"In school. My teacher is very good. But now I have this wonderful chance to talk to real Americans!" The young woman seemed oblivious to the fact that her father's car had smashed into one of our cars when his brakes failed. She told us we would have to go to the police station, so we all turned around and headed to the nearby town. The policeman at the station was so drunk that he signed the accident report with only a grunt.

"There is no unleaded gas in Bucharest and not much regular gas either."

We had lost time and wanted to get to Bucharest before dark. As we passed through each town, we looked for a sign for the unleaded gas needed for our German cars. One station attendant said we could get unleaded gas in Bucharest. We thought we could make it to Bucharest but no farther. Once we found the hotel that Dr. Urziceanu reserved for us, we parked the cars making sure to lock the steering wheel with a security "club." At this point, we did not think finding unleaded gas would be a problem. That is, until our hotel receptionist said, "There is no unleaded gas in Bucharest and not much regular gas either." The angst began to settle in.

Early the next day, we all took taxis to the university where we were to speak. We visited Dr. Urziceanu's clinic first. Dan, our musician who met our team in Bucharest had wondered what his role would be on our team. He soon found out.

We stood with Dr. Urziceanu and her staff at the back of the room as Dan played his guitar for a little boy. While Dan played, the boy watched him intensely. When the boy spoke to Dan, I saw tears running down the cheeks of the staff. I knew something really, really significant had happened.

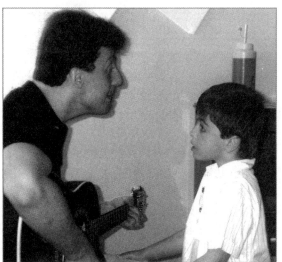

"Playing the guitar and piano are like second nature to me," Dan told us later. "However, to play while looking into eyes that hold nothing but innocent wonder . . . it was

one of the most profound and humbling experiences of my life."

Staring nose to nose, he held my face in his hands. Although there was a language barrier, a connection was made. Afterwards, he came up to me . . . and said something to me in Romanian and walked away. I turned to the translator who had a look of total astonishment. She translated his words. 'You have made me very happy today.' He was nine years old and this was his first sentence."

Dr. Urziceanu's staff served us a lunch of open faced salami and cheese sandwiches. After we finished our lunch, Dr. Urziceanu wanted Fred and me to meet the president of the university. She led us through several hallways and upstairs to the administrative offices. Upon entering the president's office and being introduced, he invited us to be seated and immediately launched into a lecture about Romanian and global politics that lasted for a good fifteen minutes. He barely stopped to catch his breath as he talked on and on. Finally, when he took a breath, I thanked him for his warm welcome and we backed out of his office. I was happy to get back to our team and to begin our afternoon seminars.

Once again, we were surprised by a large crowd at the university. The group asked many questions but was not as strident as the group in Oradea. The next day, Dr. Urziceanu took us to an orphanage for the blind and to a hospital that was being renovated as a residence for mothers and their handicapped children. After seeing so many handicapped children, I was emotionally exhausted. Furthermore, besides missing my mother, I began to worry how we were going to get enough gas to continue on our mission and eventually return to Munich.

After seeing so many handicapped children, I was emotionally exhausted.

"I will make some phone calls to find out where you can get gas," Dr. Urziceanu assured us. "The director of the hospital for handicapped children that you just visited has family connections to Peco, Romania's only petroleum company."

We held our breath as Dr. Urziceanu made the phone call.

"Yes, she will arrange for you to get gas at one particular station on the edge of Bucharest. Do you have enough gas to get there?" she asked.

"I don't know, but we will try," Fred said.

As the drivers left, we hoped the station would have enough gas to fill up all three cars. A few of our team went sightseeing. Carolyn and I returned to our hotel rooms to pray.

Carolyn wondered if she would ever get out of Bucharest and be with her family again. I halfheartedly said, "We could fly out of Bucharest back to Munich." Of course, that idea was quickly dismissed. We were responsible to drive the cars back to Munich. Carolyn's passion for the welfare of orphaned babies brought her to Romania, but now she was questioning the wisdom of being here. I felt responsible for her distress, but I could not assure her everything would turn out okay.

Finally, I prayed, "God, You brought us here. We want to do Your will, and we want to trust You. Please give us a sign that this will turn out good and that we will have gas for our cars."

Carolyn and I decided to go to a nearby porcelain shop to look for gifts for her family. While we were there, the clerk of the shop whispered, "Be careful."

Just as I looked around, a Gypsy man with his arm covered with a newspaper was moving his hand toward Carolyn's fanny pack. "Carolyn. Watch out!" I shouted as I grabbed her and pulled her away. The thief ran out of the store. Carolyn was shaken, but she completed her purchase.

Our day shopping in Bucharest was proving to be more eventful all the time. Silently I prayed that God would give us a better view of the Gypsies. I knew they weren't all thieves. As we walked by a flower stall, a Gypsy lady reached out with a lovely bouquet of brightly colored flowers.

"Let's buy some flowers to cheer up our teammates," I said.

We delighted in this poor but generous woman.

As I started to pay for the flowers, the lady said, "Today, two for one." She handed me a second bouquet of flowers. I offered to pay for them as well, but she waved her hand and said, "Nu, nu." Amazing! She smiled and we smiled back. We delighted in this poor but generous woman.

"Carolyn, I'm sure these flowers are a sign. We're going to get gas," I said confidently. We were excited to know what God was going to do. When we arrived back in my room, there was a note waiting for me. "We have gas! All three cars are full. Going out and will return shortly. Love, Fred." Wow! We could hardly believe it. We danced around the room and giggled like schoolgirls.

When our team met together that evening, we sang songs and praised God for the great thing He had done. His answer was a powerful confirmation that He was with us in our mission.

Fred told us that the gas station was closed when they arrived. The attendant opened just long enough to fill our three cars. Then he put out the "Nu Benzina" sign again.

His answer was a powerful confirmation that He was with us in our mission.

The rest of the trip through southern Romania and back to Oradea was hot and tiring. Oradea seemed like a much cheerier place than the first time we saw it. After a good night's rest in the Hotel Poienita, the Loving Arms team drove to Marghita the following day. Fred and I wanted the team to meet the abandoned babies in Marghita Hospital.

As a pediatric nurse, Carolyn was the most affected by the little ones she saw. After she was safely back in Colorado, Carolyn wrote: "Deep within my heart's memory is a child named Eva. In the corner crib, with great effort, an infant was trying to raise her head and shoulders off the surface of the bed. Her soft smile was a warm welcome as our eyes met. Then I saw her incredibly thin arms as her tiny hands moved toward her mouth. Her body stiffened as Karleen gently lifted her out of her bed. I cannot recall ever seeing the use of such rigidity to compensate for lack of muscle tone.

"In disbelief, I asked her age. 'Eva is fourteen months old,' I was told.

"I took my turn rocking her side-to-side, holding her little head against my shoulder. Her body began to soften, molding itself against mine, both of us grateful for even this one brief encounter.

"Last night, unable to fall back to sleep, I angrily asked, 'Why aren't those babies being fed?'

"The answer came slowly. *They are being fed, but there is no one to hold them, no one to love them. These are the ones who fail to thrive. You feared seeing these little ones, but they are the reason you came. And if you were to return, they are the ones that would bring you back to Romania.*"

At Marghita Baptist Church, Carolyn and I taught a seminar on the care of babies. The people met in a garage with a dirt floor. There was an outhouse out back. The inside of the church was nicely decorated. Polished musical instruments hung on the walls. Luci Cocis, the pastor's wife, translated for us. She whispered that Dr. Lupau was in the audience. Afterward, Dr. Lupau, an attractive, well-dressed woman in her forties, spoke to me.

"This is exactly what we need in Romania," she said of our seminar. "The mothers don't realize how important they are to their children. Besides working in the hospital, I have a clinic where mothers bring their babies. Can you come and help me?"

"Yes, I will plan to come next year and spend some time at your clinic," I responded. "I want to write some pamphlets on infant care. Perhaps I can get those translated for you to give to mothers who come to your clinic."

She kissed me on both cheeks and we promised to meet again next year.

While Carolyn and I were teaching, the rest of the team went to an orphanage and school for handicapped children Luci wanted us to see. More than three hundred boys, ages six to fourteen, lived there. Our team came back heartbroken over what they saw. The orphanage had no running water or indoor plumbing—for three hundred children!

Linda, our tenderhearted special education teacher on the team recalls: "The last thing I saw as we drove away was those forlorn teachers standing there. They begged us to come back next summer and teach them about these special needs children. How overwhelming their jobs must be. And the children—they just clung to us so hungry for affection. Their heads were all shaved to keep down the lice infestations. If there were any girls there, they looked just like the boys."

The Loving Arms team went home vowing to return to the orphanage to support and encourage the staff.

The following summer (1993) the Loving Arms team returned to the orphanage and presented three days of seminars. Some of the dorm staff sat in the back of the room looking very skeptical. I wondered if the seminars presented by our team really could be a catalyst to change their thinking.

I looked straight at them when I said, "The children should not be punched or physically abused in any way as a method of discipline." I believed many of the orphans we saw were regularly abused, but it would be years later before I realized the extent of their abuse.

The director of the orphanage spoke to me through a translator. "You don't understand how difficult these children are. These boys are crazy and incurable."

Most of the orphans were Gypsies and were at the bottom of Romanian society. After decades of prejudice against Gypsies, inwardly I questioned whether the staff could change their attitudes toward the children in their care.

Pat, the occupational therapist on our team, viewed her experience of teaching at the orphanage as positive. "Our seminar seemed absolutely on target. At first, the staff seemed unresponsive. Within minutes, however, they were asking questions and describing games they played. In reality, this was an animated group of caring people."

After Linda spoke, several younger teachers crowded around her. One teacher said, "You have changed our thinking. We must change our way of doing things." We left feeling very encouraged that some of the teachers really accepted what we taught. We longed to speak their language and to learn more about their lives in the village.

Five years after our Loving Arms team first taught in the orphanage, I learned that one of the teachers became the director of the school. In 1998, I brought her school supplies donated by people in Colorado.

She thanked me warmly and took my hand. She surprised me by saying, "You taught me in 1993 that it was not only what we do for the children's physical needs, but also what we do for their hearts."

I could not believe it. Here was a teacher, who heard us speak years ago, testifying that our Loving Arms team made a major impact in her thinking.

A decade later one of the teachers is studying to be a physical therapist, and another is now the director and psychologist for a special education school started in Marghita.

*Sometimes I've wondered
if the Loving Arms team has made
a significant difference
in the way orphans are treated in Romania.*

Sometimes I've wondered if the Loving Arms team has made a significant difference in the way orphans are treated in Romania. The needs are still great and there are still many orphans. It is easy to become discouraged. Yet I do know some orphanage workers' hearts have been deeply changed. Somewhere there are now young people who were abandoned as babies in the early 1990s. Maybe some were treated with kindness. And maybe, just maybe, they were viewed as unique human beings worthy of a smile.

*And maybe, just maybe,
they were viewed
as unique human beings
worthy of a smile.*

The most dismal institution that we saw was for emotionally disturbed boys. Children may be placed in this institution because they have wet the bed. Obviously, some new diagnostic criteria are needed. There was no playground equipment, and we did not see any toys.

Pat, occupational therapist

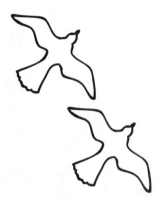

Most of the time was spent as a consultant/ assistant in the Bethesda Christian Clinic. Drs. Benjamin Pardi and Moise Mateas are caring Christians dedicated to serving Christ in their clinics. They are well trained but hampered (in 1992) by shortages of medications and modern technology. There are only two CT scan X-ray machines in the whole country!

Upon returning home, I have the tendency to look at all we have through their eyes, and I am saddened and humbled . . . it doesn't seem fair. However, the ultimate hope for all of us is in Christ, and this hope is growing in Romania like a healthy tree. We added a leaf or two.

David, team physician

◆ One hundred and sixty people
   attended the training seminars,
      representing twenty institutions.

◆ An estimated five thousand
   children will benefit from
      the training of those
         who care for them.

◆ Team members with expertise
   in medicine, education, and therapy
      worked with individual children
         and consulted with caregivers.

◆ The team delivered relief
   and educational supplies such as
      medicine, play equipment,
         an audiometer, and clothing.

9

Holding Them Close

Better to have loved and lost,
than to have never loved at all.
St. Augustine

At home in Colorado, I flip through my ever-growing collection of photos of Romania. Memories of the sights linger . . . red tile roofs, earth-colored houses, lush gardens, muddy village roads, ornate Orthodox churches, fields of red poppies, horse-drawn wagons, and sun-weathered folks hoeing corn. As the sun sets, the village houses take on a golden glow, geese and herds of cows are driven through the streets, and another day comes to an end. Indeed, each photo is like taking a step back in time.

I remember hours cuddling abandoned babies and softly singing to them. My heart will never forget the orphans I saw in Marghita Hospital. Each orphan has a unique story and special needs.

"Oh, my," I sigh at seeing the photo of one little girl. Her large, dark eyes silently speak to me of her longing to be cared for.

Each summer, from 1992–1995, Fred and I brought Loving Arms teams of professionals to Romania in an effort to improve the care of the orphans. Sadly, even after several years of training orphanage staff, the orphans' lives changed little. Even when a few of the caregivers changed their methods, this was not enough to undo the damage caused by months, even years, of neglect.

At this time, institutions responsible for child care were grossly understaffed. It became clear that, though we might not personally be able to care for large numbers of children, we could at least help a few.

All of the abandoned children displayed emotional, mental, and physical delays. A three- year-old could not stand up, a five-year-old boy had never eaten with a spoon, and a teenager stood most of the day rocking his body back and forth.

Often I asked the question, "Are the children like this because of their neglect, or were they placed in an orphanage because of their apparent limitations?"

"The children are here in the hospital because they will not be able to function out in society," a hospital pediatrician said. "And we must keep them here because they might have a contagious disease like hepatitis."

I shook my head and replied, "Maybe they are delayed because they are in the hospital and not home with their mothers. We must see how they develop with proper care." Only in later years, when a new pediatrician, Dr. Ismail Yacoob, came to the hospital did I feel that my concerns were being heard.

All of the abandoned children displayed emotional, mental, and physical delays.

For three years after our first visit to Marghita, the abandoned babies continued to languish in the hospital. The few children who were returned to their families often were brought back to the hospital after a month or two, thinner and with bruises on their little bodies. A child might be abandoned for a year or two only to be reclaimed by his parents when he was old enough to care for himself. If the birth parents showed even the slightest interest in the child, the courts would not terminate the parents' rights. Since that time, the laws regarding child welfare have improved.

Although some Romanian officials voiced concerns over the orphans' poor living conditions, change was slow in coming. The problems were overwhelming, and there were so many children in the institutions. It was beyond my grasp that any government anywhere could successfully parent large numbers of abandoned children.

Often Romanians were shocked after visiting an orphanage for the first time. To see neglected children rocking in urine-soaked beds or tied in bed was unthinkable. Many people were under the illusion that the children were treated well and that the orphanages were like well-kept boarding schools.

Thousands of children were warehoused in dilapidated buildings and cared for by staff with little or no training.

Instead, thousands of children were warehoused in dilapidated buildings and cared for by staff with little or no training. Why was the staff untrained? There are several reasons. It was cheaper to hire nonprofessionals. Just like in the US, child care is not a high priority. Also, during the communist years, information on current western research in the area of child development was not allowed in the country. Study abroad was unknown. Even nursing schools were closed, and there were no university programs in social work. The children in the orphanages were not top priority in a struggling country. Yet the children's very lives were at stake because of the deprivation they experienced early in their lives.

After our third trip to Romania, I began to evaluate the effectiveness of the big seminars. I felt restless in my heart. Was I really doing what I was called to do in Romania? I believe change comes through relationships, and even though several hundred people attended our Loving Arms seminars, I felt personally connected to almost no one . . . especially the orphans. I wondered if God was calling me to a new way of helping the orphans in Romania. My heart would never forget the abandoned babies in Marghita Hospital. Could these precious little ones be rescued? Should I return to the "place of the mourning doves" where it all began?

Should I return to the "place of the mourning doves" where it all began?

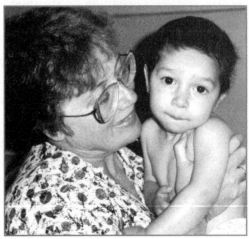

In my heart I wanted to rescue every child I saw. Yet, legally, I could do nothing. The only way I could help the orphans was to go back to Marghita Hospital on a daily basis and care for them. During the summers, many volunteers came from Sweden. We all took regular shifts at the hospital.

Whenever Barbro Gustavsson, a volunteer from Sweden, came to Marghita, she devoted her entire time to children in the hospital. "When we go to the hospital in the mornings, we find babies in soggy cloth diapers and tied in their cribs," she said. "I usually take cereal to them because often the staff does not feed them until late in the morning."

Barbro and Lars Gustavsson first came to Marghita during Christmas of 1990.

Barbro and Lars Gustavsson first came to Marghita during Christmas of 1990. They, along with their children, were faithful to come several times a year to care for the orphans.

Barbro recalls: "At night, after the last volunteer left the hospital, the children would be tied to their cribs again. After my shift, I would return to the volunteer house feeling discouraged. I knew one thing . . . the children needed twenty-four hour care in a better place."

In spite of their desperate plight, the children gave me many moments of joy. "Look! Julio is smiling!" I exclaimed. For weeks this little boy's face had been expressionless. I watched as three-year-old Eva looked at herself for the first time in a toy mirror and squealed with delight. Each step toward normalcy caused me to rejoice.

A few hospital caregivers improved their care of the children, perhaps following the example of the volunteers. One woman in particular spoke soft words of encouragement to the children. Florica, hired by Marghita Hospital, tenderly held and soothed the babies. She showed she had a heart for these little ones.

As the volunteers spent more time at the hospital, the children slowly began to respond to their loving care. They were more alert, and rooms full of infants and toddlers were no longer silent. Now more accustomed to being held, the babies cried when they were left alone. The older children grew stronger and chased each other down the hall. Hospital staff did not share our excitement over the children's increased level of activity. They complained that we were spoiling the children and making it more difficult to care for them.

Now more accustomed to being held, the babies cried when they were left alone.

To brighten the children's lives, Barbro brought donated toys and clothes to the hospital. She was puzzled when many of them "disappeared." One of the nurses complained that "the Gypsy mothers take the toys and clothes." I don't know if this was the case or if hospital staff helped themselves.

"Perhaps we are supplying all of Marghita with baby toys and clothes," I said to Barbro.

"Maybe the items are taken by women who did not have toys and clothes for their own children," Barbro replied. "Or they might take them to sell in the local market for food." Barbro felt compassion for anyone in need, even for women who stole the orphans' toys.

Fortunately, generous friends from England, Sweden, and the US continued to donate what was needed. Several foreign organizations sent volunteers to paint and decorate the rooms. Pictures were hung on the walls and toys fastened to the cribs within reach of little hands. The rooms began to look colorful and cheerful.

Even with a new "look," the orphans continued to receive minimal care. Sweet memories of progress faded away in the midst of frustrations. Anger welled up inside of me as "our children," hungry and fussy, waited for hours for a cup of unappealing noodles or a cold, boiled potato. I agonized over how the children were neglected when we were not there.

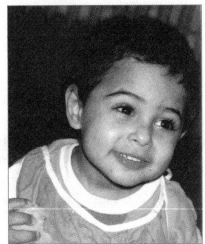

Late one morning, my surprise visit to the orphan's wing found the children hungry, wet, and tied in their beds. Frightened, little Silvia withdrew more and more into herself. I began to wonder about the more active children like Gyula, Christina, and Maria who seemed almost normal.

Will they escape before they also become emotionally disturbed?

Sometimes I felt like Alice in Wonderland in an upside-down world. The nurse, who insisted that I wear a white coat when holding the children, rinsed a thermometer in a bucket of scrub water. Children who looked well were isolated because they were "sick," while sick children went unattended. The practice of giving children injections of vitamins and antibiotics continues to this day.

Silvia, a very sick child who won Fred's attention and heart, spent most of her day in the hospital unattended, tied to a crib to prevent her from climbing out. Her first meal of the day was brought in about 10 a.m.—but sometimes as late as noon. By that time she was very hungry and chowed down food that I wouldn't touch. The food, served in a small, metal cup, varied from pieces of bread mixed with cold soup to dry, white cheese.

The young children were given bottles, but we saw no beverages for the toddlers. During feeding, the children either stood or were held. There were no high chairs, no children's furniture. The children often ate paint peeling from the walls or scraped from their cribs with their teeth. They were bruised from falling on the bare concrete floor.

Fred remembers one visit with Silvia.

She had been very sick for about a week. She clutched my shirt when I held her and walked with her. She was quiet when I sang to her "Jesus Loves the Little Children," "Jesus Loves Me," and others that I made up as we walked around the rooms. When I stood with her near the window, she became frightened and struggled to turn away. I prayed for God's Spirit to touch her and for God to surround her with His angels when I was gone.

During the first five years of our trips to Romania many times my heart cried out, *This is insane. You can't treat children like this. It's inhumane. It's a violation of human rights.* But we needed to be patient, even though we knew the children couldn't wait for the officials to decide what to do with them. Although we did see some improvement in the children's care, it was apparent that they each needed a home of their own.

One haunting memory continued to linger when we were home in the States—the feeling of a little one snuggling close and feeling loved and safe in our arms. We yearned for this memory to become reality for each abandoned child. Our dream and plea became "Let the children go" to a place of love and gentle care. In less than a year, this dream was to come true.

"Let the children go."

10

Home... At Last

> *For every child there is a season,*
> *for every child there is hope.*
> Anonymous

A solution to the neglect suffered by the children slowly emerged from within the group of us who worked in the hospital. Finally, after five long years of waiting, a series of events set into motion a new plan for the children in Marghita Hospital.

In the fall of 1995, a new hospital director was appointed. Lars Gustavsson decided it was time to speak to him. He was not only open to the idea of allowing the children to be housed and cared for in a separate facility, he gave Lars the use of a nearby building owned by the hospital as a new home for the children. Remarkable! What a joy to see Barbro's dream and God's plan unfold to give these children a new beginning. Due to an international effort, this Christian children's home would be the first in Marghita. The large building, to be named Casa Alba or "White House," would become home to the abandoned children of Marghita Hospital.

Under Lars' direction, work began late that same year to renovate the building and transform it into a home where children would laugh and play and be loved. The building was in disrepair and needed new plumbing and wiring. Walls with peeling paint and crumbling plaster were replaced with new walls for bedrooms, bathrooms, and the kitchen. Work progressed in earnest during the winter and spring months in anticipation of the day when Casa Alba would welcome the children from the hospital.

Meanwhile, Barbro and other volunteers continued their daily care of the children. Barbro prepared breakfasts of warm cereal and eggs and carried the food to the hospital.

She washed the children's soiled clothes . . . seven days a week. Renata, Florin, Marta, Attilo, Camilia, Imelda, Valentin, and Sandor thrived under this attention and care.

One of the hospital pediatricians once asked,
"Why do you waste your time on these kids?"
But now even the hospital staff realized
that these "throwaway children" had potential.

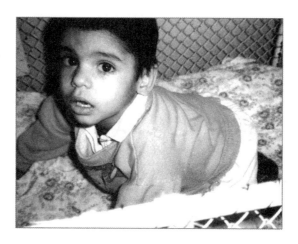

Josif
not walking
at four years.

To begin to implement their vision for the children, Lars and Barbro asked for a young Swedish woman's input in planning the new home for the children.

Iorela Karlsson had come to help the Romanian orphans four years earlier in 1992. She began as an assistant to Lars Hornberg at Caminul Felix and then became acquainted with the Hornbergs' friends, Lars and Barbro Gustavsson. Then Lars asked if she would use her artistic talents to paint Disney cartoon characters on the walls.

She agreed, and during the long hours of painting the walls, Iorela contemplated what it would mean to direct such a project as Casa Alba. She also became more acquainted with the children from Marghita Hospital who would soon move into Casa Alba. Before she realized what was happening, she was hooked. Lars, to his great pleasure, had a director for the home.

During the planning process for Casa Alba, Lars Gustavsson, Pastor Dan Micula, and Florin Costea realized that they needed to organize a Romanian foundation to be legally responsible for the work. Fundatia Crestina Elim (FCE), or the Elim Christian Foundation, was incorporated in the spring of 1996. All three men had been involved with the orphans for several years and made up the first leadership team of FCE. From 1994 on, the Loving Arms team of Mercy Ministries had focused on the needs of the orphans in and around Marghita. We joined with FCE to offer love and support to the children in Jesus' name.

Lars decided to set the opening for Casa Alba for May 20, 1996. He said we needed a deadline to make us push to finish the work. He invited Fred and me to come and help. At the time, Fred, Christine, Wendi, and I were living in Hungary where Fred taught at the Technical University of Budapest. We traveled back and forth to Marghita several times a month on weekends.

Lars decided to set the opening for Casa Alba for May 20, 1996.

I was asked by Lars to prepare the Casa Alba staff to care for the children. Lars' agreement with the director of the hospital allowed us to select the staff. Immediately, I thought of Florica, the hospital caregiver who showed a compassionate heart for the children. We also invited women from local churches to apply—those whose desire was to love the children in Jesus' name.

Thursday before the opening, I spoke to the new Casa Alba staff on "Ten Principles in Caring for Orphans." We talked and laughed together, and I sensed a spirit of excitement and anticipation among the women. Despite the fact that we were from different cultures and economic backgrounds, we really had a great time.

On Friday, volunteers joined our group, and we continued for six hours. One of the women asked if she could bring the kindergarten teacher to the training. Lars told me that this teacher was very upset with him because she had to move her class to another part of the building to make room for the children of Casa Alba. Now it was just like God to put her in my class! I expected to meet an angry woman, so her positive response surprised me. She furiously took notes, appearing to write down my every word. After the class I teased her about having writer's cramp.

"When are you coming back?" she asked. "When you do, will you visit my class?"

"Yes, I promise I will visit your class the next time I am here," I responded, happy to feel that I had made a new friend.

Two days before the scheduled opening, Fred and I went to Casa Alba to lend a hand. Tools, pieces of wood, and construction materials littered the place. What a mess! I couldn't see how Casa Alba would be ready in two days. We pitched in to clear away the clutter and then cleaned the bathrooms and kitchen.

Before we left for the night, Lars asked me, "What do you think?"
"I think there is much work to be done," I replied.
"I told the volunteers to not think. Just work!" Lars said.

We laughed, and I reflected on the determination and perseverance of this big Swede and his passionate heart for the children. In the next two days, Lars and his dedicated crew worked around the clock to get ready for the opening.

Many times in the past
I thought,

*This is my worst day
in Romania.*

On Sunday, May 19, 1996,
I had my worst day
and my best day . . .
all in one.

Fred and I offered to go to the hospital and take care of the children while the rest of the crew did the last minute work on Casa Alba. Again, my anger overwhelmed me. I hated the place the orphans had to endure . . . the filthy, smelly bathroom; the awful food that was never enough; the rags used to tie the more active children in bed. Now I knew that a new day was coming. I looked around at the cribs and longed to see them all empty.

I looked around at the cribs and longed to see them all empty.

Late Sunday afternoon all the volunteers went to Casa Alba. A few of the older children were brought over from the hospital. We had fun watching them run around laughing and giggling. Then a wonderful surprise! Folks from the local Baptist church came for a time of prayer and thanksgiving. As they sang "How Great Thou Art," I wept tears of sorrow for the terrible years of the past and tears of joy for the time to come. Before they left, we hugged and kissed each dear one.

I wept tears of sorrow for the terrible years of the past and tears of joy for the time to come.

Early the next morning, Fred and I made several hundred sandwiches to serve the guests for the "official" grand opening day. The ceremonies were set for 11:00 a.m. Lars warmly welcomed everyone, including the director of the hospital and some high officials from Bihor County. More than one hundred people gathered outside the entry which was blocked by a ribbon in the blue, yellow, and red colors of the Romanian flag stretched across the doorway. Sofia, Lars and Barbro's daughter, helped one of the older children, Christina, cut the ribbon. We all cheered and applauded our approval. As the crowd explored the building, I heard "oohs" and "ahhs" and saw smiles of admiration on their faces.

It's hard to explain the wonder of Casa Alba. Even in the US, Casa Alba would be considered a very nice child care center. Iorela stenciled bears for borders on the bedroom walls and stayed up all night to sew brightly colored curtains for the windows. The beautiful wooden beds and cribs were made by a carpenter from a nearby village. Each room was furnished with a cupboard for clothes and toys as well as three beds, each fitted with clean sheets and a handmade quilt. A plaque on each bed or crib identified a child by name. The kitchen, bathrooms, and laundry were equipped with Swedish made appliances and fixtures.

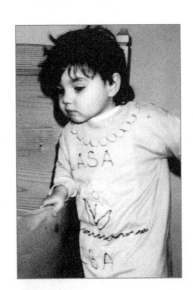

The kids absolutely stole the show!

The group gathered in the playroom. Yellow walls and Disney figures gave the room a festive atmosphere. After Lars asked for quiet, Fred offered a prayer of dedication. In his remarks, Fred described the painting we saw in an orphanage in Oradea with the caption, "For every time there is a season, for every child there is hope."

Undoubtedly, the high point of the opening was the two- to five-year-olds. They were dressed in T-shirts decorated with puffy paint by ladies from Denver's Anchor of Hope Church. The little boys looked very handsome with their hair combed and slicked down. The girls had wispy ponytails bobbing on top of their heads. Their new socks and shoes were donated by several Denver churches.

"For every time there is a season, for every child there is hope."

The kids absolutely stole the show! They acted like little angels. Fearful Sandor was able to tolerate the commotion and did not hit or bite anyone. Surprisingly enough, little Florin kept his clothes on . . . he liked to run in the buff. Sick little Silvia played contentedly on the floor. Casa Alba finally had children, or more importantly, thirteen children finally had Casa Alba.

A few days after the opening, Christine, Wendi, and other Loving Arms volunteers dressed the five babies in new clothes and carried them out of Marghita Hospital. Never again would they have to live in such dismal conditions. We rejoiced when we walked away from empty cribs in the pediatric ward. Our hope was that these cribs would never be occupied again.

> *Never again would they have to live*
> *in such dismal conditions.*

Tragically, as the weeks passed, the hospital began to fill again with twelve to fourteen abandoned babies. The health department only approved Casa Alba as a residence for twenty-four children. During the next six months, more abandoned babies were taken to Casa Alba. When Casa Alba was full, babies remained in the hospital with no place to go. To solve the problem, FCE hired three women to care for the children in the hospital. In addition, one or two FCE volunteers faithfully went to the hospital every day.

Within the year, the search for families for the children began. A total of sixty-three children were adopted in the next six years. Most of these were international adoptions, but some children were placed with Romanian families. As children left Casa Alba to join new families, there was room for the babies from the hospital, and they were moved to their home . . . at last.

Casa Alba finally had children, or more importantly, thirteen children finally had Casa Alba.

Moving to a new home is only the beginning of a process of healing for a child who has suffered the absence of loving caregivers. More has to be done, but what? Many times I asked myself, *What will their future be like? Can the best institution take the place of a family? Will the children have lasting affects from their abandonment?* Deep within, I knew the answers.

11

Blessings seldom seen

> *It is the blessing of the LORD that makes rich.*
>
> Proverbs 10:22 NASB

Brrr! Romania in January is cold. Fred and I wore our down coats and winter boots to walk on snow-packed sidewalks back and forth from the volunteer house to Casa Alba. The scenery was lovely with frost covering every tree and bush.

We had visited Marghita many times since 1991. Each time, when we left, we took with us memories of sad, impoverished children languishing in their cribs. Our photos documented the reality of the suffering. Many times we wondered, *Will we ever see conditions change for the abandoned children of Marghita Hospital? Would we ever have the joy of seeing the sparkle of life in these children?*

These questions were answered when we returned in January 1997. The children in Casa Alba were doing well . . . laughing and playing like children should. Camelia, who we never thought would walk, was toddling here and there. Sandor smiled, which was a rarity for him. Florin sat and played with a Lego train for half an hour. We rejoiced in God's blessings. God allowed us the privilege of seeing remarkable progress in the children. We brought home pictures of happy children—twenty-four babies, toddlers, and preschoolers all thriving in an atmosphere of love.

When Casa Alba opened the previous year, the Loving Arms team had trained new caregivers in the art of caring for children—children who had many problems because of the extreme neglect they experienced. All the children showed developmental delays and sensory defensiveness. We believed that better living conditions would lead to improvement in the children's health, and we knew personal interaction with those who truly care for them would stimulate their development. Even so, we were amazed at their progress in less than one year. Without the love of the caregivers, this miracle could not have happened.

Seeing the dramatic changes in the children of Casa Alba was a gift from God. We might have continued to teach Romanian caregivers in government institutions and ministered to babies in the hospital for many years and not realized such blessings. Because the problem of Romanian orphans is so huge, many nonprofit organizations have become discouraged and have left the country. But Fred and I and others working in Marghita made a long-term commitment to the children, regardless of the enormity of the problem or the obstacles in the way. We would keep coming back.

It is an awesome experience to be part of transforming a vision for the children's future into reality . . . to experience "blessings seldom seen" in one's lifetime.

Iorela was much more than the director of Casa Alba; she was mother and teacher to many of the children.

When she arrived at Casa Alba in the morning, the children would run to her and scream, "Iorela, Iorela." The first year was exciting for her as she watched the children open like rosebuds . . . little by little. During the spring of 1997, Iorela wrote her thoughts of the first year.

The first three months of this year are gone, and they left many memories in our hearts—there to stay always. There were many "firsts" for the twenty-four small persons living at Casa Alba.

Six of them took their first steps in the beginning of 1997, and it is lovely to see them grow stronger and braver each day—then suddenly let go of all support and just walk like they have never done anthing else.

Especially precious to us is that 2½-year-old Camelia now walks. Her joints are very loose, and we've been worried about her.

We have celebrated the first birthdays for five of the children, too. Not the first if we think about the amount of years that they have, but rather if we count how many of their precious birthdays that were not celebrated.

Silvia, Gyula, Florin and Renata all turned four, and Valentin three. When it was Gyula's birthday, Renata was crushed and cried "Si eu, la mult ani, si eu." "Me too, happy birthday, me too." So when her birthday came at last, she blew out the candles on the cake almost before it reached the table.

Gyula was the very first to use the fire extinguisher. He found out it was filled with lovely white "snow."

A few weeks go, Lavinia took a spoon in her mouth for the first time— a big answer to prayers for us. Until now she refused everything but a bottle. Now we're waiting for her to grow stronger.

February was a hard month for everybody. All twenty-four children took turns with the flu and had very high fevers. They were given very good care by the Casa Alba staff and are now healthy. We have a good team of workers who truly love the children and give them affection and care. Our personnel are substitutes for the parents the children never had, and they really do their work with the joy of a parent's heart.

Our children are almost all Gypsies, and for some people around us it is strange that we kiss, hug, and care for these Gypsy kids. Here, however, not only are the children loved, but they give love in return.

Mental images linger from our times in Romania. Memories of days spent with the orphans of Marghita Hospital. Claudia is an example. We met Claudia in 1991 on our first trip to Romania. Little did I realize how this once normal baby would be devastated by neglect. In 1995 she was developmentally still a toddler and still in Marghita Hospital. She could smile, walk stiffly, pick paint off of the walls, manipulate toys, and respond to loving caregivers. However, Claudia did not talk and did not look like a four-year-old. She had never been given solid food, and she was not potty trained.

As I cuddled and played with Claudia, I wondered, *Will she ever catch up, or is the damage irreparable?* Years in a loveless environment created a little girl who was at least two years behind in her development.

Claudia and her sister, Eva, looked so much alike that it was sometimes difficult to tell who was who. After one of our trips to Romania, our daughter, Christine, described Eva.

> Eva was a very special little girl to me. She is three years old. One day she was just sitting there in her crib crying. I already had my arms full with another spunky kid, but I set him down to entertain himself with a mirror and went to Eva. No matter what I tried to do, she kept on crying. Then I thought, Hey, this kid is a toddler just like my nieces and nephews. So I remembered all the games I would play with them that they loved and how I may have thought they were silly, but the kids loved them. I tried the airplane ride on Eva, and all of a sudden she was giggling like crazy.

But these girls did not forever live in the hospital. Good news! Claudia and Eva were moved to Caminul Felix where they were given hope for a new life. In Caminul Felix they live with houseparents and other orphans as a family. They will remain there until they are old enough and capable of being on their own. I prayed for healing in the hearts, minds, and bodies of these precious little girls.

Maria's story is one I will never forget, and it is still unfolding. Fred and I first met Maria in 1993 in Marghita Hospital. She was a little imp of a girl and the oldest of the abandoned infants and toddlers who suffered from severe neglect in the hospital.

When Casa Alba opened its doors in 1996, Maria was rescued She moved into her new home with her own bed and clothes. For the first time, she had plenty of food to eat. Like the other children, she ate hungrily—almost like a wild animal. In her new home, Maria was taught to sit at a table and use a spoon. She learned to live by a daily routine. In the hospital, the children had no routine and had difficulty even distinguishing night from day. During the first few weeks in Casa Alba, Maria and the other children had very irregular sleeping patterns. The volunteers took turns sleeping with the children to keep them in bed at night.

During her first year at Casa Alba, Maria was unable to talk and could be very demanding. She was obsessed with putting things in her mouth—fingers, paper, or some object she found in the playroom. Woe to the person who tried to remove whatever it was from her mouth. Her teeth clamped down hard on intrusive fingers!

A volunteer from Colorado vividly remembers Maria. "She sat peacefully in my arms. She smiled, staring into my eyes. All of a sudden, she reached up and scratched my face. What a shock to see the aggressive side of this sweet little girl."

Most important of all the changes she experienced, Maria developed close relationships with caregivers, and her heart began to know love. Linda, a Norwegian volunteer, was Maria's favorite person. Maria's eyes would light up when Linda came into the room. Maria always had a bright smile, but she was wary of strangers. It took time and effort to win her affection, but once she was won over, she gave her heart to you. Her half smile would turn into a wide grin, and her eyes would begin to twinkle as she stared into yours.

It took time and effort to win her affection, but once she was won over, she gave her heart to you.

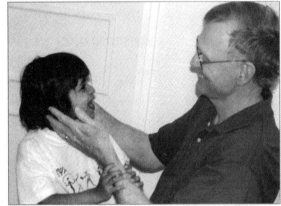

Eventually, Maria learned to count and say some words. She didn't feel so threatened by people, and she could relax. Her obsession with putting objects in her mouth disappeared. Her impulsive behavior faded away. Maria's progress would depend on where she was permanently placed. Children grow best in a family. I prayed that one day a family would meet Maria and discover the jewel that she is.

I have two vivid memories of a wonderful boy called Valentin.

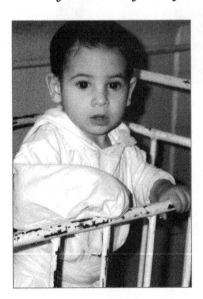

I met him in 1994 during one of our visits to Marghita Hospital. I decided to peek into one of the rooms with a closed door. I was curious to see who or what was in there. To my surprise, there was one little boy standing in his crib. He was wearing a white hospital gown and was tied to the water pipes that ran behind his crib. He didn't make a sound, but his large woeful eyes spoke to me.

I'm lonely all by myself. Come and play with me.

I talked to him and took some pictures. He never changed his expression.

So who was this boy and why was he isolated? Later I discovered that Vali had been vaccinated and the protocol was to isolate those children.

In 1996, Vali was moved to Casa Alba. During our visit to Casa Alba in 1997, I remember a more colorful scene of Vali. Gyula, a beautiful dark-eyed Gypsy boy, and Vali were sweeping the dining room floor. They seemed so proud of themselves as one held the broom and the other the dustpan. They looked like normal kids helping their mother sweep the floor. The boys were handsome in nice shirts and pants.

In less than one year we saw many changes in the children.

In less than one year we saw many changes in the children. What brought about these changes? Simple responses such a smile, touch, and conversation. These reciprocal interactions between caregivers and children, like in healthy families, were significant in helping the children to blossom. They were loved; they were safe and cared for. A child needs to have at least one person who adores him, and at Casa Alba the children have many who love them. We saw little joy among the abandoned children of Marghita Hospital. In Casa Alba, these same children were absolutely gleeful.

Valentin two years later at Casa Alba

Lavinia's first steps at Casa Alba

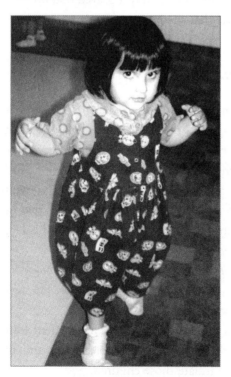

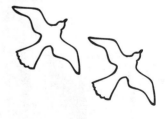

12

A Family Affair

Your life and my life flow into each other as wave flows into wave,
and unless there is peace and joy and freedom for you,
there can be no real peace or joy or freedom for me.

Frederick Buechner

From the beginning, our family has played a vital role in our ministry in Romania. The first to go with us were our two preteen daughters, Wendi and Christine, in 1992. They took regular shifts at Marghita Hospital and gave their hearts away to many of the children. The young Swedish volunteers and our daughters became fast friends. All of the volunteers came with one purpose . . . to love the children in Christ's name. And they did.

Dewey family with Romi

Our youngest daughter, Wendi, wrote her thoughts after helping to move the babies from Marghita Hospital to Casa Alba.

> Florin and Mario were two little boys I enjoyed. Florin loved to look at the mirror that we gave him and would always be putting toys in the box and pulling them out again. We would try to take him outside, but when he looked out, he would scream and turn away. Mario was much different. He was always wearing a great big smile. He was a perfectly normal kid, taking other children's toys and running away, laughing his head off. When he would go outside, you would see him run down the sidewalk and enjoying every minute of it. He will be going to Caminul Felix, the Christian orphanage in Oradea. I can't wait to go back again to see how all of them are doing. Jesus really loves the little children, all the children of the world.

Year after year, several of our children joined the Loving Arms team. I was thrilled to see our teenage daughter, Josie, get caught up in the emotions of a moment and show deep compassion for these little ones.

Josie

"The one place that affected me the most was the baby hospital in Marghita," she told us later. "I can still see those poor little babies just lying in their cribs with no one to hold them or play with them. There was one little boy that I held and sang songs to. He just stared at me with his big pleading brown eyes as tears rolled down my face. What I would have given to take him home with me."

Early in 1995, Fred spoke to me about an opportunity for a sabbatical for the following year. Ten years had passed since his last sabbatical from Metropolitan State College in Denver where he was teaching. Should he apply for another sabbatical? Should he pursue a position in Romania or perhaps in neighboring Hungary?

Wendi, Fred, Karleen, Christine

One important consideration was a school for Wendi and Christine who would be in the eighth and ninth grades. When we investigated possibilities in these two countries, we learned about the International Christian School of Budapest (ICSB), a small but growing school with a good reputation.

Fred applied to the Technical University of Budapest and was accepted for the spring semester of 1996. His sabbatical was approved, and the pieces began to fall into place. Teachers at ICSB found a townhouse for us to rent a short walk from the school, and Fred had a reasonable commute to the university from our location. And, very important to us, Marghita was only a four to five hour drive—a trip we could easily manage on a three-day weekend.

As it turned out, we made many of these weekend trips. The spring of 1996 was a busy time in Marghita. Renovation of the building for Casa Alba was progressing in earnest, decisions needed to be made regarding selection of the staff and a director, discussions with the director of the hospital and the head pediatrician were necessary, the babies in the hospital needed continual care, and a Christian foundation was being organized to oversee the work with the children. What a whirlwind of activity!

Our base in Budapest encouraged other family members to come.

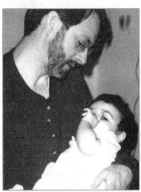

The first to visit were our son, Scott, and son-in-law, Randy Davis. During Fred's spring break at the university, we took these two young men to Romania so they could meet the orphans and see for themselves the children's living conditions. Both men were deeply touched.

Scott and orphan baby

When we returned to Budapest at the end of the week, Randy was met at our house by his older brother, Brian, who was a youth pastor for children of American military stationed in Germany. After Scott left to return home to Colorado, Randy returned to Romania with Brian. The two men went from place to place to see the orphans: babies in the hospital, school-age orphans, and older teens in Cadea.

What they saw overwhelmed their emotions

What they saw overwhelmed their emotions. Brian's tender heart was broken over the plight of young people in the government orphanage in Cadea. After returning to Budapest, Brian sat at our kitchen table and wept over the Cadea kids. Words could not describe what he had experienced.

In the ensuing years, Brian returned many times to Romania with young people and their families from military posts in Germany. These groups built play equipment at Casa Alba and the camp; volunteered to work at the summer camps; and brought needed supplies such as diapers, aspirin, baby wipes, and formula. Support from the military families in Germany is continuing years after Brian left Germany.

Play equipment built by volunteers

Scott attends a largely African-American church in Denver's inner city. His dream was to encourage minorities from the city to form teams and go to Romania to reach out to the orphans. In 2000, Scott led the first Loving Arms camp team. Planning and running a camp for thirty-five teen orphans is a huge challenge.

Mary, Scott's oldest child, was part of this first camp team at the age of eleven. Now as an older teenager, Mary goes to Romania twice a year. These experiences have touched her deeply and shaped the direction of her life.

Mary, Scott's oldest child, goes to Romania twice a year.

In one of our Mercy Ministries newsletters, Mary wrote, "When we said good-bye the last day at camp, Romi stuck his head out the van window and screamed, 'Don't forget me!' It is so sad to think of the 'home' that the kids are going back to. A home where they are beaten and have few possessions. I am happier for the babies of Casa Alba because they have more of a future and may be adopted. I will miss everyone so much."

Mary's experience caring for the orphans was so positive that soon her brothers, Ben and Christopher, joined her. Now Scott's wife, Melanie, and their three children go to Romania every year. Scott and Melanie are expressive writers and some of their observations appear in later chapters of this book.

At fifteen, Mary, began to take winter trips to Marghita. She wrote this letter to her supporters.

This winter trip was very different from our summer camps because our time with the kids was not structured. This was cool because we could spend more one-on-one time with the kids, listening to their joys, their needs, and their pain. It is so hard and at the same time so wonderful to be able to share in their struggles and to be trusted with their secrets and fears.

One of these kids is a fourteen-year-old boy named Niki.* He is very outgoing and always seems to be smiling, but underneath his cute face he holds so much pain.

Like all of the kids, he struggles with the shameful hurt of being abandoned by his parents. But he had become very attached to two of the year-round volunteers, and they became like the parents he never had. Last year they had to leave Romania for medical reasons. For Niki it was like being abandoned all over again.

Now, more than a year later, he is still deeply broken by these abandonments. He says his favorite music is sad music because it makes him think of all the important people in his life that he has lost, and it helps him express the sadness he feels.

None of us can heal all of the pain these kids have, but we can be a friend who they can trust, someone to hold them and love them through it all.

While some of our time with the kids was serious, a lot of it was crazy and fun. We had a wild New Year's Eve, Romanian-style!

We took twelve kids out of the orphanage and the girls from one of the group homes to FCE's clubhouse for food and games, and then we had a worship and prayer service at our apartment.

Then we went out into the center of Marghita and set off fireworks! There were explosions everywhere, raining down from the balconies of the

*Not his real name.

apartments overhead and under our feet as kids set them off, screaming "La multi ani" Happy New Year! It was dangerous and exciting and so much fun.

After we recovered from New Year's Eve, we took a trip to Oradea with five kids from the orphanage. Oradea is the nearest major city, about an hour away from Marghita. We took them to McDonald's and saw the latest Harry Potter movie. It was awesome to be able to spend time with them outside of the orphanage and watch them loosen up and enjoy themselves.

When we weren't at the orphanage, we were hanging out with the kids in the Christian group homes. These homes were started by the foundation that we partner with. Each home has six kids, either six boys or six girls, and two houseparents. It is so amazing to see the transformation that the kids go through as they are taken out of the abusive situation in the orphanages. This change was especially apparent in one of the girls at the girl's house. She used to be the toughest, hardest girl in the orphanage. She had so much control over the other kids that we called her the "queen." But, just in the last few years, she began seeking relationships with the foundation volunteers, and she has completely turned her life around. The other girls look up to her and go to her for help and advice. It was such an encouragement to see my new friends thriving in their new family.

One of our older daughters, Karyn, was completing her master's degree in physical therapy at the time we moved the children to Casa Alba.

Several weeks after the chidlren were moved, Karyn came to Marghita to begin physical therapy programs for children who were delayed in their development. Two years later she returned to follow up. We were amazed at the response of several of the children.

Later, revealing her excitement, Karyn reported Lavinia's remarkable progress.

Lavinia sleeps in a crib.

Her caregivers try to feed her in a high chair every morning, but she only drinks milk. She is just learning to crawl and is just beginning to babble when you play with her.

You might picture her as a typical six-month-old. But Lavinia is not a typical child. She was abandoned at Marghita Hospital and is almost three years old.

Lavinia spent the first year of her life with almost no human interaction and now has to be taught things most babies learn on their own.

I have worked with Lavinia for three weeks now. I taught one caregiver how to help her strengthen her legs and how to teach her to walk. I had a special chair built that would help her muscles to develop and make it easier for her to learn to stand.

Last night, I brought the chair over and put her in it. Then I took her hands and helped her stand up and take two steps!!! She is still a long way from walking and may never be a typical three-year-old, but those two steps gave me a sense of being part of a very special beginning in this child's life. Whatever family God has for her future, I hope they will learn like I did that when she smiles at you, it is pure gold.

When she smiles at you, it is pure gold.

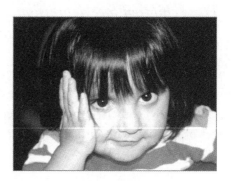

By the time Wendi was in ninth grade she had traveled to Romania many times. During these trips, she really developed respect and camaraderie with the other volunteers. In a 1997 Mercy Ministries newsletter, she wrote about her experiences.

> It's so good to be back and see the kids grow. With the Swedish volunteers and our Loving Arms team's help, they have improved. These kids can change with love and care! The people here love the kids so much. Some of the Swedes stay for three or four months, while others stay year-round. They trust God for the work that's being done in Marghita. Even though many of them have hard times and miss home, they are willing to come. Please pray for them and the Romanians who work here ... they need it. All of them are so sweet -- they gave us a going away party on our last night.

There is no way to completely describe God's hand on this place.

When we tell family and friends about the orphans in Romania, many want to come. There is no way to completely describe God's hand on this place. It has to be experienced. Since 1991, more than one thousand volunteers have come from Sweden, Norway, Finland, the UK, Germany, Canada, and the US to Marghita to care for the children and to help with construction projects, teaching, preaching, singing, and everyday office tasks. They are mostly young adults, but some have chosen to spend their retirement years in Romania in ways that are of eternal value.

These children have been damaged emotionally, mentally, and physically, and the task is not easy.

These children have been damaged emotionally, mentally, and physically, and the task is not easy. The disappointments and failures, but also the joys, are keenly felt. We often ask ourselves, *Can this particular child be rehabilitated?*

These children face depression, anger, violence, impulsiveness, self-mutilation, and obsessive/compulsive behaviors.

These children face depression, anger, violence, impulsiveness, self-mutilation, and obsessive/compulsive behaviors. What causes such profound differences in how orphans behave and relate to others? And what keeps so many of us coming back to face the challenges of working with difficult children in a foreign land?

13

True Grit

True Grit: The actions of a person who moves forward toward his goal in spite of the obstacles in his path.

Though it may not be so pretty here, I love it." With tears in her eyes these poignant words were spoken by a young woman who volunteered for many years in Romania and was returning home to Sweden for her wedding. She and her fiancée worked together with teen orphans and fell in love. It was time for them to return home and work in their professions. Six months after they were married, they returned at Christmas for a visit. The children they learned to love will always remain in their hearts.

> *Why so much dedication?*
> *Why do people go to stay for years*
> *and then return for visits?*
> *What is the "hook" that attracts these volunteers?*

I believe the answer is that God places in our hearts a desire to do important things of eternal significance. We go as strangers to this land, unfamiliar with the Romanian ways and feeling very vulnerable. About this time, we meet some enchanting children who need someone to love them. We bond very quickly to the children and to other volunteers who share our experience. After all, we are in this together, fighting for the same cause.

In the fall of 1995, Lars and Barbro Gustavsson decided they must be in Romania full time in order to make a difference in the children's lives. They moved to Marghita with their children, Sofia (20), and teenagers, David and Par. Their original plan was to stay for only one year. Now they could begin to see their dream of Casa Alba become a reality.

The first months were very discouraging.
Barbro remembers her feelings during this time.
"Oh, it seemed like there were problems all around
that we could not find a solution for."

The first months were very discouraging. Barbro remembers her feelings during this time. "Oh, it seemed like there were problems all around that we could not find a solution for. Often the people we worked with had many problems in their own personal lives. It was difficult for them to also help the children."

Several years before in 1992, Lars had rented a house for the volunteers which they called "Herculane" because of the name of the street where it was located. The house was small with two bedrooms and a kitchen and dining room combination. A dozen or so volunteers slept in bunk beds in one bedroom, and the Gustavssons occupied the other bedroom that also served as their office and a meeting room. We had one bathroom and only a few hours of water per day.

The young folks liked to stay up late and watch movies, and we older folks liked to go to bed early. Of course, we would get up early while the younger ones wanted to sleep in. In spite of this, Herculane was cozy and we had a family feeling together. We enjoyed wonderful prayer and worship times usually in three different languages—Romanian, English, and Swedish. In time we became so many that the long-term volunteers began to rent their own apartments.

We enjoyed wonderful prayer and worship times
usually in three different languages—
Romanian, English, and Swedish.

The first year the Gustavssons lived in Marghita was full of challenges and went by fast. In the fall of 1996, at the end of their first year in Romania, Lars and Barbro faced a difficult decision. Should they go home or stay in Romania? Finally, realizing they were needed in Marghita, they decided to stay. Lars sold his prosperous landscaping business in Sweden and the Gustavsson family moved into their own apartment. Herculane continued to be used as the volunteer house. Casa Alba was opened and running smoothly under Iorela's direction, so the Gustavssons began to focus on the older orphans.

The next project was the renovation of the rundown orphanage building in the village of Cadea. The Cadea orphanage was a "mean" place where the toughest kid was "boss." After the first phase of the renovation was completed, the boys destroyed the bathroom sinks and toilets. As winter set in, Lars agreed to continue the work only if the director would heat the building. The director's promises soon gave way to excuses. Throughout the winter, the building was freezing inside. The cold winds blew through broken windows into the rooms.

> *The next project was the renovation*
> *of the rundown orphanage building*
> *in the village of Cadea.*

Barbro; her daughter, Sofia; and Cici, a young Swedish friend, visited the orphans at Cadea almost every day. Often Barbro would bake a cake to celebrate a boy's birthday. Later, when girls were brought to Cadea, the women took turns sleeping there to protect the girls.

The Cadea orphanage was a "mean" place
where the toughest kid was "boss."

During this same time two other Swedish young women, Linda and Louise, began to volunteer at another government orphanage for three hundred children ages six to sixteen. The two women were overwhelmed with the needs of so many children. As these volunteers were beginning to reach out to the older children, others continued to care for the abandoned babies in Marghita Hospital.

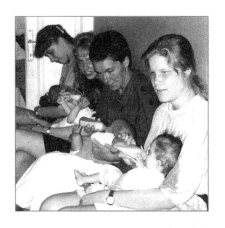

*Ohers continued
to care for the
abandoned babies
in Marghita Hospital.*

In June of 1998, a group of thirteen boys "graduated" from the Cadea school and orphanage. Graduation did not mean successful completion of the trade school program. It simply meant the boys had turned eighteen and had to leave the orphanage. Abandoned by their families, they had no place to go. Lars decided he could not let the boys go out on the streets to be beggars or worse. He spearheaded FCE's plan to establish transit homes, or halfway houses, where the boys could learn about family life from houseparents and acquire job skills. The first transit house was not yet ready, and the boys from Cadea were desperate.

Our FCE team felt the impact of the pressing needs of the children who were in the care of the foundation, and trying to prioritize our efforts was stressful. In one planning meeting, I suggested that the foundation should focus on the younger children because we had a better chance of success with them. Lars rose to his feet, and with great emotion punctuated by his large size, exclaimed in a quiet voice, "I cannot leave these boys out on the streets. I cannot!"

"I cannot leave these boys out on the streets. I cannot!"

Lars was determined, and he convinced the director of Cadea to allow the boys to stay until the end of August. After that, no one knew what would happen to them. In August, the director apparently ran out of patience, packed the boys into a van, and dumped them on the main street in Marghita.

What could be done for these boys? An answer flowed from the hearts of three dedicated women—Barbro, Sofia, and Cici. The women decided to live with the boys in a rustic camp in Padurea Neagra, or the Black Forest, until the transit house was ready. The camp, then owned by Marghita Hospital, is located in the Transylvanian mountains an hour's drive from Marghita. Before the revolution, hospital personnel and their families vacationed there. Now the empty camp buildings were in a state of disrepair and without heat or water.

The boys only knew an atmosphere of violence and stealing. Years of living in fear of being beaten or violated deeply affected them emotionally. They needed time to heal. Food and other supplies were purchased, and two van loads of boys were taken to the camp in the Black Forest. There was no kitchen and only a rickety outhouse to serve the needs of the group. The boys had to carry water from a spring two hundred meters away for drinking and washing. Everyone was apprehensive about the arrangement, but living on the streets was the only other option for the boys. Barbro and Lars were determined that this would not happen.

The boys only knew an atmosphere of violence and stealing.

For the women, there was a certain sense of adventure. What did God have for them during this time with the boys? Barbro, Sofia, and Cici knew these boys and felt perfectly safe. Coming from the violent surroundings at the orphanage, the boys soaked up the kindness and affection the women offered.

Before long, the leaves began to be tinged with autumn colors. The clear blue skies accentuated the tree-covered hills. The stream that runs by the camp sparkled in the little sunlight that filtered through the dense covering of trees.

All too soon, winter set in with all of its beauty. It also brought a freezing chill to the enormous concrete building. After one of the boys cleaned the floor with water, ice formed, and they all had great fun skating in the hallway. Lars brought two small space heaters which they used in their sleeping rooms.

They passed their time repairing the building, sleeping, and talking. In the evenings, they gathered around a heater, and the boys shared their painful lives with the women. When they could no longer keep their eyes open, Barbro moved quietly from bed to bed to pray with each of the boys before they fell asleep. The little group lived there from September to February.

One of the older boys, Zoli, became like a son to Barbro. She, as well as Sofia and Cici, modeled a mother's love and kindness. Zoli recalls, "I liked being there in that small camp." For the first time, Zoli had a family.

In the mid-1990s, one special young man came from Sweden and stayed for months at a time. Pierre not only loved children, but he could fix anything. I used a VCR in teaching child care classes, and when it jammed, I called on Pierre to get it working again.

Several years went by, and I did not feel like I really knew Pierre. One day when we were walking from Casa Alba to the volunteer house, I asked Pierre about his childhood and his family.

He told me that when he was a baby, he had a medical condition that required surgery to insert a shunt to drain fluid from his brain. If the tube gets blocked or if there is an infection, he needs immediate medical attention.

"Do you think you can get that medical help here?" I asked.

"No, probably not."

"But if the shunt gets blocked, then what would happen?"

"Well, I could die."

As we continued down the street, I wondered what his parents thought of him being in Romania. "I think it is amazing that your parents are willing to let you come," I said.

"Yes, and I am an only child."

After Phyllis Parker's husband died in 1997, she sensed God leading her in a new direction. She joined several of our Loving Arms teams to go to Romania to care for the orphans. The defining moment for Phyllis came three years later.

After several short visits during the previous two years, in the year of 2000, I sold my hair salon, my house, and my car, and I moved to Romania. Many thought I had lost my mind to give up all my security and possessions to go to help a bunch of orphaned teens. The farewell with family and friends was difficult. I knew I would miss the abundance of the US.

I taught hair styling to eight teens in the state orphanage in Cadea. What a horrible place. Just ask me about the bathrooms there. In an empty room, I prepared a makeshift "salon." I needed to teach in peace, away from the gangs who roamed unsupervised through the dark halls. My students first practiced on mannequins and then with live models. I expected a lot from class. I told my students they must be showered every day. As it turns out, they only had warm water on Fridays. There are no seats in the bathroom and seldom any water to flush. Often we had to do shampoos with cold water. God showed me what it was like for them . . . all the time.

At times, an orphan would reject Phyllis' instructions and react in anger. One young man responded, "You can't tell me what to do. You don't know what it is like to be an orphan. You have a car and a house. We have nothing." That student went on to be one of the most skilled at styling hair. Another teen cried, "I just can't do this; I'm not good enough." He ended up dropping out of the program.

*Imi became a
skilled hairstylist
thanks to Phyllis.*

Phyllis is thankful to God for helping her love orphan teens and for providing the opportunity to use her skills. After living in Romania for three years, she describes her spiritual journey.

*I have the joy of seeing homeless teens give their hearts to the Lord.
I have learned to work with other Christians for a common purpose. I have
worshipped the Lord with an international body of Christ. There is a deep
bond between the volunteers that will never be broken. I have such a sense of
being in God's will. Whatever I gave up is rubbish compared to the rewards
of loving children. The joy and happiness I experience can never be
duplicated with possessions.*

One day I received an e-mail from Alisha Inch, a preschool teacher in British Columbia. She read about my ministry with FCE in the Christian women's magazine, Virtue. The article touched her heart, but she had never thought of becoming a missionary. Alisha put the article aside and forgot about it. Two years later, a missionary visited her church and encouraged Alisha to consider a short-term missions trip.

"But where? What country?" Alisha asked God. While praying one night, Alisha heard God say, "Romania."

The following day, she rediscovered the clipping from *Virtue* magazine and immediately wrote me an e-mail full of questions about FCE's ministry with Romanian orphans. I responded with answers to her many questions and suggested she contact Courtney Brown, a volunteer from Colorado who lived in Marghita, for firsthand information. The two women e-mailed back and forth. Courtney's enthusiasm was contagious, and she encouraged Alisha to move ahead with her plans and go to Romania.

The obstacles were formidable, yet God works through the impossible.

"Consider I had no money to buy a plane ticket," Alisha said. "But, by God's grace, I met a Christian travel agent who charged my ticket on her personal credit card. Predeparture bills needed to be paid, but I had no savings. A $300 gift from my church paid them all . . . with one penny to spare."

Mistakenly, the agent booked her ticket for Bucharest, Romania. When she called to tell me her itinerary, I said, "No, Alisha. Bucharest is twelve hours by car from Marghita. Change your ticket to Budapest, Hungary. From this airport it is only a four hour drive to western Romania and Marghita."

The challenge of preparing to go to Romania was like no other for Alisha. She had to completely trust God. In October 2000, Alisha left for Romania. Florin and Courtney met her at the airport in Budapest. Alisha writes:

It is all a blur. Riding to Marghita, I began to freak out. Florin drove fast down a two lane road. I wondered if we were lost. I pretended to be asleep while on the inside losing it. My mind whirled as I thought, What the heck must I have been thinking to do this?

After a night of troubled sleep, Courtney and I walked to Marghita Hospital. My first impressions were of the smell of urine, the sad eyes, and bare cement walls. I went back to Herculane and cried, wanting to go home. Finally, I thought I could tolerate three months and then go home.

One night, I dreamed I stood fighting a war . . . a battle. Then I realized that a spiritual battle raged all around me. I knew the enemy sought to discourage me. At the end of two months, I felt God had something else for me to do, but I didn't know what. My heart longed to be involved . . . I just didn't know how.

On one of Alisha's free days, a volunteer from England asked her if she wanted to meet some of the older orphans at another orphanage. She doesn't know why she said yes.

The Dacia, a Romanian made car, broke down on the way, but I will never forget our visit. It changed my life. I knew God called me to those children. This is it . . . what God wanted me to do. My heart and life were ripped out by God. I knew I would come back.

When I went home, so much was going on in my head and heart. I didn't want to talk about it. To me, it felt like I might be going crazy. I felt angry at people and their attitudes. I went to see an elderly missions pastor. He told me, "Alisha, this is normal." God used him to speak peace to me, and I could rest even in my sorrow.

Not only did Alisha come back, but she stayed five years and added a wonderful foster son to her life.

Hundreds of volunteers have gone to Marghita, and each has a story about how God worked in their lives. I hope some will write their own book. Going to Romania to love orphans is a significant marker in our lives. It is a time when we gave up the comforts of home and left our families to join with others to bring God's eternal hope to the abandoned children of Romania. The volunteers are people of faith with "true grit" who have stayed the course in spite of the obstacles they encountered along the way.

14

What Is Wrong?

What milestones have passed in the confines of the pediatric ward with no caring mother or father! . . . The cuddling, the finger play, the rocking, the child has been denied. All of these things that encourage attachment and normal brain development in infants, and which start them on their way to developing conscience, have been lacking.

Foster Cline, M.D., *Uncontrollable Kids—From Heartbreak to Hope*

What is wrong with this child?" I asked as I held my first Romanian orphan. She felt stiff as a board. Her muscles tightened at my touch. Even though fully acquainted with the results of child neglect, I was shocked. It is one thing to understand the theory behind the problems of neglected infants and quite another to hold an unresponsive baby. The experience is like no other. A helpless and hopeless feeling overwhelmed my emotions and I moaned, "Oh, God, help me. Help me know what to do."

In 1991, my heart broke and remains broken to this day. I believe God wants me to always be brokenhearted over the plight of these little ones. I believe He wants me to work with passion to bring hope for their future.

Because of my educational background in early childhood development and my experience with orphans, I was in a unique position to help others understand the problems faced by motherless children. While we know children can be resilient, rejection by their mothers deeply wounds them emotionally. The very person who should be there for them . . . isn't. I asked, *Why? Why would a mother give birth and then walk away?* Can a woman lack emotional strength to care for her baby . . . the flesh of her flesh? Can she be so empty inside to be persuaded that the State will be a better parent?

A pediatrician at Marghita Hospital told me he found a baby in a heap of rags in a cold house. Such deep poverty is beyond my experience. But providing the basic necessities of life is not enough. A mother must have inner resolve to care for her child and emotional support from those around her. Without these elements, a woman does not function as a normal mother.

The following scenario describes the circumstances faced by many young women in Romania.

A young pregnant woman is poverty-stricken, malnourished, abused, and addicted to alcohol or drugs. The traumas she suffers are passed to the baby growing inside her body. Her daily stress level remains high, which in turn stresses the developing baby. The mother is drained emotionally, and she is not prepared to go through the pain of childbirth. Often the baby is unplanned, and she may resent this unwanted new life.

When her time has come, she gives birth in the maternity ward at Marghita Hospital. The baby is small and frail. She thinks maybe something is wrong with him. She thinks of her home life and cannot imagine caring for the baby there. Surely, she thinks, the baby will be better off in the hospital. So after she has regained her strength, one morning she goes for a walk in the courtyard and decides to return to her village without the baby. She is Gypsy and is registered as living in a nearby village. When a social worker goes to the village to look for her, she has moved and no one knows where.

The little one, let's call him Mihai, never experiences the softness of his mother's breast. He never hears her whisper his name. He never sleeps in the comfort of her arms. He cries with hunger pains. Hours go by, and no one comes. Finally, someone puts a nipple to his mouth. But many babies must be fed, and no one has time to hold him close as his mother would. The milk comes out of the nipple too fast for him, and he chokes. This is just the first of a multitude of assaults. When his eyes start to focus, there is no color for him to enjoy. No smiles for him to respond to. There is no joy in life at all.

He cries with hunger pains. Hours go by, and no one comes.

During this time, billions of minute neurons in Mihai's brain are scrambling to get organized. We might think of the brain as being hardwired for sending messages to the rest of Mihai's body. Stimuli such as colors, sounds, touch, food, physical movement, and smiles give the neurons tracking paths. The awful problem is that Mihai does not experience any of these stimuli routinely. Yes, someone might speak to him, but then long hours of silence may follow. With time, neurons that aren't being used slough off.

With good intervention and adding stimuli to his daily experience, other neurons can take over. But as one of a dozen or more abandoned babies in an understaffed hospital pediatric wing, good intervention is not possible. Mihai must stay in the hospital until his parents are found and relinquishment papers are signed. Then a protective shelter such as an orphanage must be found. If he is one of the lucky ones, he will go to Casa Alba even before he is legally free. If he is not so lucky, he will go to one of the state orphanages for babies.

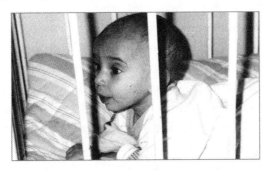

Some years ago, I visited one of those orphanages. Over five hundred babies and toddlers lived in this grossly overcrowded institution. As the director showed me floor after floor of babies, I wanted to say, *Don't show me anymore. This is sickening.* The place was clean, but in some rooms one caretaker took care of twenty children. As in any country, the State is a poor parent.

The scenario of baby Anna, born into a caring family, is very different.

The scenario of baby Anna, born into a caring family, is very different. Anna is given smiles and cuddled by many willing arms. She is fed when she is hungry, and her diapers are changed when she is wet. She is rocked . . . back and forth. When she is fussy, the warmth of her mother's touch calms her. She makes little noises, and her mother notices them. Her mother talks back to her in a soothing voice, and she in turn gives her mother a big smile and continues to babble. Her needs are met . . . her world is okay. She can relax because she is safe. All these simple events give this baby a good foundation for life.

This nurtured baby's neurons in the brain are connecting and developing pathways. She has gained a great deal of knowledge in her few months of life. From the sleepy little bundle that she was at birth, she is able to respond to the people in her world. It's a fun world where people make her giggle, count her toes, and never let her go hungry. Her mother takes note of developmental milestones when she begins to roll over and play with her feet. At five months she can sit up and move around on the floor. One developmental stage after another follows.

If Mihai, the neglected baby, is still in the hospital, he lies in his crib and stares blankly at the ceiling. He does not have chubby legs and arms. In fact, his skinny little arms and legs barely move. And when they move, they flail in jerky motions. He doesn't smile because no one has smiled at him. He could be learning to sit up and take solid food, but he is given only a bottle with watery gruel. His pale skin gives testimony to his malnutrition. It may take Mihai a long time to learn to walk because he cannot sit up. He has not learned to put weight on his hips. In fact, he lies still because his body has made an indentation in the crib mattress. He does not have the strength to move to another position. If his legs spread froglike, he will be much delayed in walking. With therapy, he might walk by the time he is two or three.

> **His pale skin gives testimony to his malnutrition.**
> **It may take Mihai a long time to learn to walk**
> **because he cannot sit up.**

Mihai's world is very different from Anna's. He experiences anxiety when people are around him. He is afraid of many things. A bath is a fearful time because he is roughly bathed in cold water. There is no hot water. Once he dropped his bottle on the floor, and one of the nurses slapped him. Now he is afraid when someone holds him. He doesn't know if they will be kind or will hurt him. He knows his world is not a safe place. He must be vigilant at all times.

It doesn't matter that he is very quiet. No one worries that he isn't talking. As he grows and is more mobile, he will be tied to his crib with rags. His most painful experiences are the injections. He receives injections of large doses of antibiotics and injections of vitamins on a regular basis. The needles are large, and seldom is there anyone to comfort him. Just another reason to be fearful.

> **It doesn't matter that he is very quiet.**
> **No one worries that he isn't talking.**

If Mihai goes to Casa Alba, he might later go to a foster family. If he does not go to Casa Alba, he will likely go to a state orphanage with hundreds of other babies and toddlers. As he gets older, the chances of Mihai being adopted are slim.

Even at the tender age of two,
Mihai learns
in the orphanage that it's
a mean world out there.

Even at the tender age of two, Mihai learns in the orphanage that it's a mean world out there. If he doesn't hold tightly to his bottle, another stronger child will take it. When visitors come, he grabs a leg and reaches for the stranger's hand. He desperately wants what all the children want . . . to be in someone's arms . . . anyone's arms. But a bigger child pushes Mihai away. He cries, but the visitor moves to another child. When he is bigger, he will be one of the strong ones vying for the attention of a stranger.

At three, Mihai is sent to another orphanage. Finally, he is walking. The caregivers think maybe Mihai is mentally retarded because he took so long to learn to walk. They are sure this is why he is an abandoned child. They think he is damaged and can't be fixed, so they spend little time with him.

The orphanage is cold in the winter with very little heat. His nose is always running. He cries a lot and sometimes is spanked to get him to stop crying. It doesn't help. But he is learning to be tough. Only the tough survive in an orphanage, and he will survive. He begins to steal whatever he can find. He steals from the smaller boys. Why should they have something when he does not? When he is caught, he is beaten with a stick. Now he hates with a vengeance.

Now he hates with a vengeance.

This fictional saga is representative of a great number of children. When they are older, we wonder what is wrong with them. The ones who are adopted often exhibit aggressive behaviors learned in their early years in an orphanage. They feel empty inside. One adult orphan described herself as feeling like a person carrying a half empty bucket around all her life.

For a small number of children, this feeling of never getting enough combined with rage often leads to violence. They are a heartbreak to those who try to help them. They are afraid to be open and to be loved. They are anxious when others are in control. For them, the only way to be safe is to be in control of others around them.

Psychiatrists call this phenomena reactive attachment disorder (RAD). Tons of books are written about boys and girls like Mihai. Therapies are in place to help adopted children who come to the US and other western countries.

Parents who adopt and are unaware of their child's background might soon ask, "What is wrong with my child? He doesn't make eye contact, he is not cuddly, and he does not respond to hugs and other attempts to be in close physical contact. He can be very charming to others but throws tantrums when he can't have his own way. Often he destroys a gift he was given." Frequently a mother will comment, "The other children are afraid of him."

The next question an adoptive or foster mother might ask is, "What am I doing wrong?" A mother may feel like a failure because all children "should" respond to being nurtured. The mother of an abandoned child may feel "to blame" for her child's rejection. However, she must realize that she did not cause the problem. Her child was damaged from severe neglect. Parents of a child with attachment problems also need to know they are not alone. There are many other adoptive parents who are observing the same behaviors in their children. It does not matter what country the orphans come from. They all are affected by the absence of loving caregivers during their formative years.

But all is not hopeless.

It takes loving relationships plus time, energy, and God to retrain an orphan's brain to feel loved, to accept nurturing touch, and to believe he can trust people. For some children this may be accomplished in months; for others it may take years.

One of my adopted sons is in his thirties. Finally, he is realizing that he wasted a good part of his life resisting close relationships because he did not feel safe with anyone. The abusive ordeals he experienced as a child imprisoned him. The unrecognized inner emotional pain kept him from being a loving and responsible adult. Now his heart has softened. In the future, he has plans to share his story with Romanian orphans. Fred and I feel encouraged, but we had to wait a long time for love to break through the walls he built around his heart.

To see a well-adjusted orphan is a time to rejoice. A few children are able to maintain a sweet spirit in spite of day-to-day humiliation in an orphanage. These children are at one end of a continuum. Other orphans are adversely affected, but with help from specialists who understand reactive attachment disorder they will make remarkable progress. At the other end of the continuum are the ones who have hardened their hearts. True, the healing process may be painfully slow for them, but we must never give up hope. God is part of their story, and the last chapters of their lives are yet to be written.

15

A Mother's Heart

There is in all this world no fount of deep, strong, deathless love,
Save that within a mother's heart.

Felicia Hermans

id you think we would come?" I asked the nervous and excited young woman holding her two-year-old son.

She smiled and said, "I had hope."

Her brown eyes glistened as we watched Loving Arms team volunteers, Pam and Amy, both occupational therapists, gently examine frail, little George. He did not resist their careful, probing fingers, but he kept his eyes glued to his mother's eyes. Pam's and Amy's cheerful smiles brought results . . . George smiled back. His flailing arms responded to their touch. As I watched, I knew that this little boy understood the language of love.

I knew that this little boy understood the language of love.

"He has cerebral palsy, but I know we can help him," Pam said soberly. "His mother is obviously very dedicated to him, and he is responsive. We can teach her some exercises that will encourage his development."

Thus began this unusual encounter with a mother named Crina and her son in a remote village in western Romania. The story of the crossing of our paths is more than intriguing. I would say it was a divine appointment.

In January 1996, after our family had moved to Budapest for six months, our Mercy Ministries' office in Denver received a letter from Romania. It was addressed to no one in particular . . . just to Mercy Ministries. Since it was written in Romanian, no one in the office knew the nature of the message. When our son, Scott, came to Eastern Europe in April, he brought the letter with him. Of course, we couldn't read it either, so we kept it until we could find someone to translate it. The letter was put with some other mail and almost forgotten. In May, a Romanian friend came to Budapest and stayed with us for a few days. I remembered the letter, and I asked him to translate it.

A mysterious letter . . .
an unusual chair . . .
and a story of
"divine appointments."

He said it was from a woman named Crina who lived in a village not far from Marghita. She was writing about her small son, George, who was not yet two years old. She described him as spastic and slow in his development. They lived in one room with her husband's family, and she asked us to please come to her village and help her son.

That summer Pam, Amy, and Zacharia, a Romanian friend and translator, went with us to visit two villages where we knew families were struggling to care for their handicapped children. First, we visited a mother with seven children, three of whom were handicapped. Later, we arranged for surgery for the baby with a club foot and a special school for his older sister who was deaf.

Sometimes we see
a mother
who loves her
handicapped child so
much that she cannot
part with him.

When we arrived at Crina's house in the second village, Zacharia knocked on the door. Crina opened the door and Zacharia told her who we were. Crina was so excited and nervous that I thought she would go through the ceiling! Thus, we were given the opportunity to meet this wonderful mother and her son.

In Romania, we see many abandoned children.
Some have been abandoned because they have
handicaps, while others appear to be perfectly normal.

In Romania, we see many abandoned children. Some have been abandoned because they have handicaps, while others appear to be perfectly normal. Tragically, some parents have decided to let the State parent their children. They think the children will fare better in an orphanage where they will have a warm place during cold winter months and be well fed and cared for. In the villages, there is pressure on a family to place their handicapped child in an institution. To many Romanians, having a handicapped child is a disgrace.

However, sometimes we see a mother who loves her handicapped child so much that she cannot part with him, and we are excited and encouraged. She may be poor and have no resources, but she is determined to care for her child. Sadly, she may face ridicule from family and friends. But in her mother's heart, she knows her child should be in her arms. She knows that if he is to progress at all, it will be in her tender care.

> ### To many Romanians,
> ### having a handicapped child
> ### is a disgrace.

During this first meeting with Crina, we quickly realized she was a marvelous example of this kind of mother. George's movements were jerky and uncontrolled, but it was very clear to us that he was attached to his mother. His blue eyes would search for hers. Once he could focus on her, his world was okay.

Pam and Amy measured George from every angle. They said if we could get a carpenter to build a special chair, George could sit up. Then Crina would not have to hold him all the time. When he grew out of the chair, another would have to be built. Pam and Amy gave George some toys specially designed for children with his problems to help him with his coordination. They told Crina they would come back the following week and teach her some exercises for George.

After Pam and Amy finished their evaluation of George, Crina asked her mother-in-law to come into the room to meet us. Entering the room with the older woman was her severely retarded nineteen-year-old daughter who also lived with the family. I could tell that this girl was defiant and very difficult to care for.

> ### Fred asked if we could pray with them,
> ### and they readily agreed.

Fred asked if we could pray with them, and they readily agreed. The mother-in-law was visibly touched by his prayer and our concern for the family. She offered to serve us dinner but we graciously refused.

Before we left, I had one question I was dying to ask. "How did you know about Mercy Ministries?"

Crina said last year a friend took her child to see Dr. Lupau, the pediatrician at the health clinic in Marghita. Dr. Lupau and I are friends, and I had given her our *Mama* and *Touch* booklets to distribute to young mothers. Crina's friend gave her a booklet with the Mercy Ministries' Denver address on the back. In January 1996, Crina decided to write us, hoping we would respond. And how surprised she was when we did!

One more amazing piece to this story . . .

One more amazing piece to this story is about the special chair for George. When we went back to Marghita, we told Lars about the need. He said some folks in Sweden had made a strange donation. He went to a storage shed and pulled out an elaborate metal chair, equipped with cushions and straps. Pam and Amy were stunned. Not only was the chair perfect for George, but it was adjustable. As George grew, the chair could grow to accommodate him.

"This chair would be very expensive in the US," Pam said. But here it was . . . just waiting for George.

So do you believe in divine appointments?

So do you believe in divine appointments? Well, I sure do . . . and I think Crina believes so, too!

> *In this you greatly rejoice, even though now for a little while,*
> *if necessary, you have been distressed by various trials,*
> *so that the proof of your faith,*
> *being more precious than gold which is perishable,*
> *even though tested by fire,*
> *may be found to result in praise and glory and honor*
> *at the revelation of Jesus Christ.*
>
> 1 Peter 1:6-7 NASB

16

Orphan Life

*I know the feeling of hugging, but I also know
the feeling of being thrown away as a useless rag.*
Zoli Farkas

Fred and I sat in a barren orphanage play yard with no play equipment. We heard a ruckus behind us. Two teenage boys chased a young girl and knocked her down on the sidewalk next to the school building. One boy punched her in the mouth and viciously began to kick her in the head. Fred quickly jumped up and chased the boys away. The girl bled from her mouth and held her hand over her ear. She cried in Fred's arms for about twenty minutes.

The greatest tragedy is that four adult staff stood over to one side and none of them made any move toward her. When I told one of the regular volunteers, he sighed and said, "Such is life in the orphanage."

It is truly surprising when one of these kids is able to lead a normal life after so much abuse. Yet some do . . . like Zoli.

In 1994, Zoli captured our attention. He stood out from the other boys in several ways. Zoli was easy to talk to because he spoke English rather well. His thick, curly hair gave him the appearance of being taller than the other boys. He always looked clean and neat.

Rarely did the boys have their own possessions, including clothing. In the orphanage, clothes and shoes were heaped in one large pile in the room of one of the boys. When one of the boys needed something, he dug through the pile and pulled out whatever might fit. Of course, this resulted in an outfit of mismatched clothes. The laundry was done infrequently, and few boys relished washing their clothes by hand. Therefore, clean clothes were not a common sight. Cleanliness is difficult when there is limited running water and certainly no hot water.

Yet Zoli's appearance was not his most striking characteristic. It was his kindness toward the younger and smaller boys. He refused to allow the harsh conditions of orphan life to destroy his spirit. It was his resiliency of spirit that impressed me the most.

Zoli refused to allow the harsh conditions of orphan life to destroy his spirit.

In the early 1980s Zoli was placed in a large orphanage for toddlers, Leagan de Copii, in Oradea. He spent his first years with hundreds of other toddlers in this institution. At the age of three, officials moved Zoli to an orphanage in the village of Beius.

In 1994, when he was fifteen, Zoli ended up in the vocational high school and orphanage in the rural village of Cadea. Presumably, the trade school taught the boys livelihood skills, particularly farming and machinery. Unfortunately, the staff did not understand orphans and made little effort to teach them anything. In fact, the teachers told me they were happy when the children did not show up for class. They viewed the children as incapable of learning. The buildings which were used for classes were largely empty of students. Furthermore, the orphans were not taught to take care of the farm animals at the school. These chores were left for paid workers. Zoli wanted to go to a better academic high school in Oradea, but the director of Cadea said he was in no position to send him there.

At age seventeen, Zoli wrote his story, which he called "Orphan Life."

Orphan Life

Orphan life means hard experiences that can be difficult to forget or leave behind you and continue your life. No one wants to be an orphan or live an orphan's life. It consists by tears and pain and might even become your death. You are forced to live alone and you have to get what's necessary to stand the situation.

Children that grow up in their families become educated, but children from orphanages don't have anyone that cares for them, which accordingly means that they feel useless. In our world it might be different, but don't worry, in God's eyes we are all valuable people. What I mean is that I sometimes think that a child from an orphanage has the possibility to love and understand problems easier than the children that grew up in their families.

My mother left me right after I was born. I grew up in an orphanage and I really know the meaning of pain. I know the feeling of hugging, but I also know the feeling of being thrown away as a useless rag. I still remember a lot of things from the different orphanages I've been to. I remember the big boys that forced us younger boys to give them our food and money. They sometimes beat us and forced us to go out on the streets to beg for [a] certain amount of money that they needed.

The years went by, and I came to Cadea. I lived there and studied for three years. Before I got there I had dreams about Cadea, how nice I thought it was, and I thought that I really should enjoy my stay. But when I came to the boarding school, all my dreams flew away. I shared the bedroom with seven other boys. When I walked in, I saw a cold and empty room. I got a mattress and a broken bed. It was cold [with a] cement floor and the glass was missing in the windows. It was September. The winter arrived and it was still the same. We had no heat and only one blanket each. We got sick many times during the winter. Besides I got sick in my appendicitis and had to be operated. Many people came to see me. I was very happy for all the boys from Cadea that visited me. Then I realized that I meant something for them. In the hospital I also started to think a lot about life, how short the life is and I wondered how I came on this earth.

When I came back to school I started to find out if I could get any information from my birth certificate. I got a name of a village, which I visited. I could not find my mother there but the neighbors knew what town she moved to. I went there with opened mind and many questions. How does she look like? What will she say?

When I got there she was not at home. I waited, and when she finally came, I saw the neighbor running to her. I heard him saying, "Come, there is someone here that wants to see you, maybe it's your son?" I felt very emotional when I asked, "Are you Etelka?" She answered "Yes!" I asked if she knew about a boy called Farkas Zoltan that has been in an orphanage. She answered that she did. With tears in my eyes, I told her that I am her son and how I finally found her after all these years.

With her eyes full of tears she hugged me and said, "Forgive me for leaving you but I didn't know what to do. I was poor, your father was often drunk and it was a really hard time. I divorced him but I didn't have any food or money, so I thought it would be much better for you if I leave you in an orphanage."

I realize now why she left me and how hard it was for her. I can understand her. I have three brothers and one sister. May God bless us all.

While at Cadea, Zoli planned once-a-month birthday parties. He wanted to help the children have fun times. Zoli and the children loved disco parties. The tougher ones taunted Zoli about reaching out to the younger children, but he pressed on with determination. When they realized how much the parties filled him with joy, they backed off.

For growing teenagers, tea and bread for breakfast, watery soup for lunch, and bread for dinner did not satisfy their needs. They were constantly hungry. When the water to the building was shut off, which happened frequently, the teens had to melt snow for drinking water. Incredibly, the building had no heat in the cold Romanian winter.

> *For growing teenagers, tea and bread for breakfast,*
> *watery soup for lunch, and bread for dinner*
> *did not satisfy their needs.*

Out of the darkness of Cadea, one light shined on Zoli. Irina, the orphanage nurse, cared about the orphans and nursed them when they were sick. Zoli remembers that she traveled by train to Oradea to buy clothes and soap for them. Irina encouraged the boys to plant and tend a vegetable garden and to clear the field in front of the orphanage for soccer. The other staff avoided the boys. The person in charge at night often locked himself in his room, leaving the boys on their own. Cadea was a dark and dismal place in the daytime. The night could be terrifying . . . drinking, beatings, and rape.

College students from Oradea who served internships in social work at Cadea quickly gave up on these kids, never to return. These teens were tough. Just the word *Cadea* created fear. With only a few exceptions, like Zoli, these boys seemed unreachable.

> *Cadea was a dark and dismal place in the daytime.*
> *The night could be terrifying . . .*
> *drinking, beatings, and rape.*

In the summer of 1996, Barbro, Sofia, and Cici turned their full attention from Casa Alba to the boys at Cadea. Nothing prepared them for the challenges they were about to face. When Sofia gave one teen a T-shirt and tennis shoes, everyone demanded the same. When Cici befriended a younger boy, some of the older boys threatened to beat him.

Some of the boys were very good at picking locks. No lock was secure for very long. After the boys unlocked a car door, they stole whatever they could carry. At one point, Sofia and Cici told the teens they were leaving and would not return until they respected the volunteers and their cars. After two weeks, they received a package of letters from the children. In letter after letter, the children begged them to come back.

> *In the summer of 1996, Barbro, Sofia, and Cici*
> *turned their full attention from Casa Alba*
> *to the boys at Cadea. Nothing prepared them*
> *for the challenges they were about to face.*

Zoli had become good friends with Sofia and Cici. He was disappointed when they stopped their visits. He recalled that he did not know what to write, but he felt that he wanted to try. In his letter, he wrote that he did not understand why they came because he knew the orphans were tough. He asked for their forgiveness and wrote that if they would come back, he would help them. Zoli says Sofia and Cici must have relied solely on God's strength when they finally decided to go back.

At the end of 1995, girls were sent to Cadea. The volunteers thought this was extremely unwise. The boys already had enough problems. The girls acted tough and talked like boys. They had short haircuts and wore boys' clothing. It was hard to tell the girls from the boys.

> *At the end of 1995, girls were sent to Cadea.*
> *The volunteers thought this was extremely unwise.*

The orphanage staff thought they could keep the boys out of the girls' section at night by installing an iron gate in the hall and locking it. It took the boys only a few minutes to pick the lock. Younger girls were sexually assaulted. A few of the older girls were stronger than the older boys and could protect themselves. However, some of the orphans paired off for physical pleasure with one another. I found it amazing that there were no pregnancies from these liaisons. Perhaps a pregnancy ended with the baby aborted. The truth may never be known. The policy of sending girls to Cadea ended in 1997.

In one way the arrival of the girls improved the situation. They liked to participate in the fun times. Zoli arranged contests, parties, sports, and dances with karaoke. The orphanage provided no recreation equipment to keep the teens occupied. Zoli gave Sofia and Cici a list of what he needed, and they returned with the supplies and equipment.

Trusting in anyone, even God, was difficult.
He had to fight with himself to believe God loved him.

Many times the boys went to church in Marghita. When he was eighteen and it was time to leave Cadea, Zoli felt he needed help from God. He listened to the preaching in church and understood that with God he could manage. Zoli says he struggled with this process of change and a growing faith in God. Trusting in anyone, even God, was difficult. He had to fight with himself to believe God loved him.

In 1997, Lars Gustavsson planned to establish
transit or halfway houses
for the boys who finished school in Cadea.

In 1997, Lars Gustavsson planned to establish transit or halfway houses for the boys who finished school in Cadea. Each house would have "parents" to teach the boys how to live in a family. One year later, the first transit house in Marghita was completed. An enthusiastic young couple, Vasile and Mariana, was chosen to be houseparents. They took in Zoli and four other boys. At first, everyone behaved and Zoli had no problems with the other boys. But as time went on, the boys became quarrelsome and less cooperative. When Zoli tried to be good, another boy would taunt him with, "Are you better than me?" Eventually they learned to work together and be a family.

One of Zoli's best memories of living in the transit house was Christmas. With snow drifting down, the family sang Christmas carols and exchanged gifts. He felt happy inside and had a good time. In the orphanages, staff did not celebrate Christmas or birthdays for the children. During the Christmas holidays, the staff went to be with their families. They left almost no provisions for the boys . . . only bread and certainly no Christmas gifts.

The spring of 1998, we took our daughter-in-law, Melanie, to the Black Forest to see where we planned in the future to have the summer camps. Some of the boys, including Zoli, were there with Barbro. Since Zoli could speak English, Barbro suggested Zoli ride back to Marghita with us. As we bumped along, Zoli talked with Melanie who was traveling with us.

Melanie tells of her conversation with Zoli that day:

> My most moving experience [in Romania] has been a conversation with Zoli. An orphan from Cadea, he is now 18 and one of the five young men living in the transit house. He speaks exceptional English. Recently, he explained, he met his mother for the first time. She told when he was born and how she left him at the hospital. "And I understood," Zoli said. "But she was so sad. It was easy to give me up when I was small. But now that I am big she sees what she gave up."
>
> I explained that I had been adopted and that I would probably never meet my birth mom.
>
> "You don't have her address?" he asked.
>
> "No. Or her name. Nothing but the name of the hospital," I said.
>
> He reached out and touched my arm. "Oh," he sighed. "I am sorry for you." To have a young man who experienced so much loss express such real compassion for me . . . a point he can deeply relate to . . . it is a gift of God's care for me. I hope it meant something to Zoli, too. To feel the touch of Jesus through this young man is a privilege.

Almost a decade after we first met, Zoli is a handsome, well-groomed twenty-five-year-old man. In 2003, as I sat and talked with Zoli, he told me more details of his life story.

One day in 2000, Florin Costea came to the transit house to see Zoli. Florin had a ministry to the orphan teens for several years and now served as the Romanian director of Fundatia Crestina Elim (FCE). He came to the transit house to tell Zoli that a family near the city of Cluj wanted to help an orphan boy, and this was an opportunity for him to live with a family. Zoli had three days to decide if he should leave.

Zoli remembers, "I asked Florin how I could decide?"

"He said, 'Ask God if you are to leave. If it is God's will, then leave.'"

Everything changed for Zoli when he moved to his new family. At first he thought it would be wonderful to be part of a Christian family. Yet Zoli did not feel accepted. For so many years as an orphan, people treated him as worthless. He constantly fought with himself to believe people liked him.

Most of the people in the church appreciated Zoli's willingness to help wherever needed. He assisted with the church services and got on well with almost everyone. Several members, however, did not think a Gypsy orphan should participate in the church services. Since Zoli had never been a regular attendee in any church, he was unaware that he might not be welcomed by some.

Zoli found a job at a wood products factory operated by a man and the man's mother. Zoli didn't understand which one was his boss, and he was frequently given conflicting instructions. When his relationship with his boss continued to worsen, he decided to seek the advice of his pastor. After listening to Zoli, the pastor talked with some of the village people, and he learned that many others also had problems with Zoli's boss.

> *So now Zoli lived with a family that did not accept him,*
> *was rejected by some church members,*
> *and he had problems with his boss.*

So now Zoli lived with a family that did not accept him, was rejected by some church members, and he had problems with his boss. Because of his inner struggle with self-worth, the problems became insurmountable for him. After a year, he couldn't take it any more. He went to Marghita and told Florin the whole unhappy story. Florin came to the village and spoke to Zoli's family. The parents said, "We asked for the best boy. Why didn't you bring him?"

The pastor invited Zoli to come and live with his family. Zoli's new family seemed to understand how to encourage him, and he began to feel like a worthy person. One day, his pastor looked at him and said, "I don't care what you have been, you are a good man."

Zoli enjoyed living in the village. Most of the people accepted him even though he was a Gypsy orphan. Some of the old people looked after him like he was their son. For the first time, he felt he was living a normal life.

At the age of twenty-one, Zoli moved to the town of Huedin where he found a better job in another woodworking factory. He moved into his first apartment, a very small place with only a kitchen and bedroom. Thankfully, the people of the community and the church welcomed him.

> *Zoli was serious about his faith*
> *and became active in the church.*

Zoli was serious about his faith and became active in the church. He led the prayer time and reading of the Scripture. Later, he told friends, "A person who is nothing can be somebody and can help others around him."

Zoli told me the story of his love for a young woman. After praying for some time to be able to meet someone he could love and marry, Zoli became acquainted with a young woman at church named Maria. He liked her very much, and she expressed similar feelings for him. Zoli and Maria were very happy when they were together.

Maria was a student at the university in Cluj. Her parents became concerned about her relationship with Zoli, and they tried to put an end to it. They said they knew Maria best, and if she had a boyfriend, she might lose interest in studying.

Zoli was crushed. He went to her parents to ask why they rejected him. To his disappointment, they refused to discuss their daughter with him. They were angry with him for even thinking of dating their daughter. When they saw him in church, they smiled and were friendly, but later he heard that they spoke badly about him in the village. Deep inside, Zoli was sure of the reason. He was a Gypsy orphan. Reluctantly he and Maria decided to maintain a distance. With a sigh, Zoli said, "Maybe someday, they can see that someone who was nothing can be something."

> *They were angry with him*
> *for even thinking of dating their daughter.*
> *Deep inside, Zoli was sure of the reason.*
> *He was a Gypsy orphan.*

I asked Zoli what he sees in his future. What does he dream about?

After a thoughtful pause, he said he might want to study theology and be a pastor or a missionary. He wants everyone to know that they have value.

Zoli wants to tell young people to honor and respect each other. He heard one girl say, "I had a relationship with a boyfriend so I cannot be clean again."

He responded, "Yes, you can be clean again. All you have to do is ask God for forgiveness. God makes you new. Sins are forgiven and forgotten. It was a problem for me to believe I was forgiven. Now I know that I am forgiven."

> *Zoli wants to tell young people*
> *to honor and respect each other.*

When he was twenty-three, Zoli finished night school. It was his dream to go to the University in Oradea. Some people were shocked when they heard about his plans, but others encouraged him. "Oh, you can. You can."

Some day, Zoli hopes to marry and have his own family.

I believe he will do just that.

*"A person who is nothing
can be somebody
and can help others around him."*

Zoli Farkas

17

Lost Boys

I know there is love from God. I know!
Barbro, Lars, the Christians . . . they saved my life.
They love me and teach me how to work.
I try now to tell the other boys about God.

A young man who is an orphan

Fred and I met Imi in 1994 when he was fourteen. Imi has large, dark, laughing, though sometimes brooding, eyes. He used those eyes to con unsuspecting Americans into believing his woeful stories. Of course, I spoke little Romanian, and Imi did not speak English. One day, as we communicated with gestures, Imi pointed down at his shoes. They were men's leather shoes about four inches longer than his feet. I did not see how he could play volleyball or soccer with a pair of shoes like that. He looked at me with pleading eyes and said, "Mama." Okay, I nodded my head yes. I would find him a pair of shoes.

At the volunteer house back in Marghita we had a storage area full of clothes and shoes for the children. I rummaged through hundreds of shoes and finally found a pair of Adidas that looked like the right size. The next day, we brought the shoes to Imi. He tried them on and seemed very pleased with them.

When I saw him again, he had the old leather shoes on. I pointed to his shoes asking with my eyes where his tennis shoes were. He shrugged and looked at me with big, sad eyes. I thought one of the bigger boys had stolen them and he feared tattling. Later, I learned he sold them in the market to get money for cigarettes.

Imi is a creative businessman. In the years to come, I would learn much more about Imi and witness more of his creativity.

Imi still has those same dark eyes. When I look into his eyes, I see the hope that he has in his life. Yet his eyes also speak of sadness and anger. I sense he will always carry the scars of orphanage life. During Imi's teen years, he lived in the Cadea orphanage—a place run by the toughest teen survivors. Something similar to the pecking order rule in William Golden's book *Lord of the Flies*. If you were a little boy, you did not cross an older boy who was the "boss."

> *When I look into his eyes,*
> *I see the hope that he has in his life.*
> *Yet his eyes also speak of sadness and anger.*

The miracle is that Imi did survive, and for one reason. He met Jesus Christ as his Savior in Cadea. Barbro, Sofia, and Cici visited almost daily and shared their faith in Jesus with the orphans. The children's response did not come overnight. At first, they were skeptical. Why would someone want to come to Cadea just to be with them? This puzzled the kids. In time, the boys and girls realized that these volunteers came because they loved them. That made them curious. Why did the volunteers love them? Those questions offered a perfect opportunity to share the love of Jesus. Love won the day. Many of the orphans became believers.

> *The miracle is that Imi did survive,*
> *and for one reason.*
> *He met Jesus Christ as his Savior in Cadea.*

This orphanage is where Imi felt love for the first time. Learning to love and trust another person transformed his life. Formerly withdrawn and brooding, he emerged into a new world like a butterfly from a cocoon.

I first met Tomi during Easter week in 1996. Our Loving Arms team invited a group of orphans from a nearby orphanage to come to the volunteer house to dye Easter eggs. We brought plastic Easter baskets and grass so that each child would have a basket to take back to the orphanage. We had no idea whether the staff or the big kids would take them.

One group of boys, ages ten to twelve, was so excited about the project. I could see the delight in their eyes as they dyed their eggs. I don't think they had ever done it before. Tall and skinny, Tomi gave us big smiles and enthusiastically decorated his eggs. We all ate jelly beans and, even though we could not speak Romanian, we laughed together and enjoyed ourselves.

As time passed, I forgot about Tomi. I didn't know that he spent most of his teen years in the orphanage. I met him again eight years later at the camp for orphans in the

Black Forest. He had finished the eighth grade in the "special school" at the orphanage and continued with high school in the village. For me, the biggest surprise came when I heard Tomi speak nearly perfect English. He served as one of our translators at the camp. Now a handsome young man, Tomi played the guitar and loved to lead the worship songs during the evening meetings. After dinner, we had many long talks. He told me about his life as an orphan.

"I have been in an orphanage almost my entire life."

"I have been in an orphanage almost my entire life. How did I get in an orphanage? Simple, my parents divorced. They separated from each other in a different district. And this is how it happened. When I was born, my father was obligated by the state to pay to my mother a 'family allowance.' He came and took me from my mother with force. He put me in the hospital in that district without any concern over what would happen to me. In that time, you could die from starvation or something worse could happen to you. So it was like I was being sent to die. In that time many babies died of starvation, or it happened many times that they disappeared without somebody to know."

"Did your parents ever come to visit you?" I asked.

Tomi leaned forward and lowered his head as if ashamed. "I did not see my mother until two years ago. I found a file that said I stayed in the hospital for six months, and then I was moved. I cried so much for my mother . . .

"I was told that 'you were abandoned' in the hospital and your parents almost tried to kill you by leaving you in the hospital. In that moment, I saw my life was of no value, without hope and love. I remember when I was six or seven years old, I tried to take my life by jumping from a balcony from three floors. Nothing happened to me except I was taken to the hospital."

"I saw my life was of no value, without hope and love."

During our conversation, Tomi's emotions seem to alternate between grief and anger. His life was full of incredible loss and sadness.

I asked Tomi to e-mail me and tell me more about his life in the orphanage. This is what he wrote.

A life in an orphanage is something that nobody will wish to go through. It means a life without love and hope. A life where you have to fight all the time to survive. A life where you know starvation. A life where people make fun of you. A life where you are scared very much.

I remember my life was so hard. The conditions were unimaginable. You were treated like something of no value. It was like you were condemned for something that your parents did. I remember one time, I ran from the orphanage without asking permission. I did not know where to go. I just wanted to go far away from that place. Life was not meant to be that easy for me. Of course, I was caught by the staff who works there. I remember how hard they punished me. They beat me with a stick. The beating was so hard that I could not stay on my legs for a couple of days.

Well, the years passed and I was moved to another orphanage. I was happy when I was moved with hope that I will be moved to a better place. The place was the same. I stayed there a couple of years. Then I was moved to another orphanage ...cold Bratca. The life there got a little better because there were some British people from England.

Finally on our faces you could see smiles and happiness.

After a few more years, in 1994, I was moved again. Here at the beginning, when I came, it was like my first orphanage. The conditions were so bad.

Tomi lived in so many different orphanages. The constant moving from one place to another would be confusing for a young child. I would guess that each place had its own set of rules . . . and consequences for a child who broke those rules. Furthermore, friends and familiar caregivers were left behind. Each time Tomi was moved, he endured more loss. Can such a child ever be whole again? Tomi's outlook changed dramatically as loving people came into his life.

After knowing Zoli, Imi, and Tomi for so many years, I thank God for His grace that filled the boys' lives with love. I don't even want to think about where they would be without the godly volunteers who came to love them.

"Rejoice with me, for I have found my sheep which was lost!"
Luke 15:6 NASB

18

A Whale of a Ride

by Scott Dewey

O ye Whales, and all that move in the Waters,
bless ye the Lord: praise him, and magnify him for ever.

Book of Common Prayer

Her hair is pulled back smoothly in a bun. She has the olive-brown skin of a Gypsy and the kind eyes of a mother. She wears a long, green nurse's smock with large pockets.

She cares for orphans in a place called the Sanctuary. She is holding a small boy, stroking his hair. His forehead is damp, and his eyes roll backward. She holds his arms from flailing. She looks into his face and whispers a low, soft song. It is late, and when

he finally has fallen asleep, she lowers him into a wooden crib. Looking around, she snugs blankets over a couple of the other children and lets herself out of the door.

There are other women with her. Some are laughing. Some are bleeding. They are running now, these green-smocked women, rushing together down the cobblestone streets of the village. From what they are running, or to what, I cannot tell, but they desperate, like horses running for the barn—legs pumping, chests heaving, dodging oxcarts, bursting around corners into the alleyways, slipping, and splashing the mud, straining forward. All of them are bleeding now, badly, from old wounds and new. They are bleeding from their pounding feet and bleeding from their hands. They gallop ahead, bleeding from their sides too, blood soaking through their smocks. Everything is a rush of rain and sweat and red and muck and hair and hard fast breath and . . .

I sit up. It is dark, but I can see my wife, Melanie's, face on the pillow. I look at the clock, take a sip of water to calm myself, and ease back under the blankets.

Wide-awake, I wonder what it was about. Not just the dream, but also my whole trip to Romania. The trip was not much different than I thought it would be, or was it? I had seen the pictures of abandoned children and heard the stories. Being there was worse than the pictures, but I expected that. What I didn't expect were those troubled nights back home.

> Wide-awake, I wonder what it was about.
> Not just the dream, but also my whole trip to Romania.
> Being there was worse than the pictures, but I expected that.

What am I going to say Sunday evening at church? It is amazing, actually, how interested everybody is. I had imagined I would come back wanting to talk about it, and no one would care. As it turns out, everyone cares, and I don't want to talk about it. I don't really even want to think about it. But I do, especially when it is quiet and dark.

I wonder who won the Rockies game? They might have rallied after I turned it off and went to bed. I suppose the postgame coverage is over by now, but maybe I can find a talk show. Rush, there's always Rush, I guess, or Larry King—I haven't listened to Larry King in years. Maybe with the volume down low, so it won't wake Melanie . . .

I am going to have to get those slides in order in the tray. They are all mixed up. The Marghita babies, tied into their cribs, are in with shots of industrial waste and crumbling infrastructure. The Gypsy wagons should go with the mountain scenery and handicrafts, I suppose, rather than with the city shots of beat-up buses and electric trams. The orphanage bathrooms with no toilets, only holes in the floor . . . For my church presentation I should take out the slides that show excrement. There are the plates of Wiener schnitzel, fit for princes, prepared for us and the Sanctuary children by the women in green smocks. The little church in Abram with the wood-burning stove. The pastor's wife who cried when she told us about finding the orphans. It is all in a jumble, in the tray and in my mind.

> I think of my children, all three, asleep upstairs.
> I see their faces, mingled with the faces of the orphans.

Lying here on crisp sheets, I think of the ripped-up mattresses for the teenage kids at Cadea. I look again at Melanie. I've tried to tell her about Romania, but it's been hard. She says I haven't told her much. I've told her what I could, but I suppose she is right. Yes, she knows; I haven't told her much.

**Lying here on crisp sheets,
I think of the ripped - up mattresses
for the teenage Kids at Cadea.**

I think of my children, all three, asleep upstairs. I see their faces, mingled with the faces of the orphans—a jumble I must sort out too. Bright eyes, blank eyes. The fearful silence from the chain-link cribs; the safe, rambunctious chaos of our living room. Christopher, toddling full-tilt through the house, waving Mary Beth's report on killer whales wildly aloft. "Stop him, Benny, stop him," Mary Beth yells, and in the ensuing tangle of arms and legs, the crumpled prize is retrieved. The breakfast banter, the run for the bus. We're slipping and sliding down the sidewalk. My mind is slipping and sliding now, too, and I think I'm getting on the bus, but I don't know where we're going. The trees and houses are floating by.

"Killer whales are excellent hunters. They can swim at speeds up to thirty miles per hour. They are also excellent aquarium performers, and can be trained to do tricks with people on their backs." Mary Beth finishes her presentation, and there is applause from her teacher and classmates. I am next up, with my slide show. People are listening politely.

"Romania was ruled for twenty-five years by a tyrannical dictator named Nicolae Ceausescu. His policies left the country in economic and social ruin. He was overthrown in 1989, but the suffering continues. One tragic legacy of his rule is a half-million or more orphans, most of whom are severely neglected and locked away in state institutions."

**The encyclopedic tone helps.
A few more facts and figures, perhaps . . .**

I'm doing all right. The words flow clearly; the knees are firm. The encyclopedic tone helps. A few more facts and figures, perhaps, and then for added color an anecdote or two about Vlad the Impaler, ruler of Transylvania 1456-1477 ("yes, *that* Transylvania, yes, Dracula and all"), or about the even more twisted Ceausescu, with his homicidal secret police loonier-than-fiction propaganda films.

"The purpose of our trip was twofold." I do need to move to the point. "First, to bring love and care to the orphans. To hold them, speak to them, clothe them, and feed them. In short, to give them what God intended every child to have—but what these children haven't had. Second—and this, we hope, is a goal with even more far-reaching impact—to train and equip Romanians themselves to care for the children."

It is quiet in the church now, and dark. I fiddle with the focus knob. Unsure of my knees, I sit down.

It is quiet in the church now, and dark.

"As you can see, the children abandoned in the attic of Marghita Hospital are tied into their cribs. They have remained in this tiny room for years with virtually no human interaction or stimulation.

"As you can see, the children have eaten the paint off of the metal bars and chain-link wire covering their cribs—maybe out of hunger, or simply distracted boredom. Until people began visiting recently, they have had little food and no toys.

"As you can see, many of the faces are bruised. Children left alone for long periods develop self-stimulating behaviors such as hitting themselves rhythmically with their fists.

"As you can see, many of the children—even older ones—lie with their legs flayed out to each side, limp. They have never had occasion to try to crawl or walk.

"As you can see, this child stares blankly at the ceiling, and reacts only by shielding his eyes when someone approaches.

"As you can see, this girl is bald. Severely disturbed, she has pulled her hair out with her hands.

Can you see that it is worse than you can see?

"As you can see . . ." Can you see that it is worse than you can see? But the faces on the screen are gone, and Pastor Roberts is blessing the broken bread.

Some of us are humming along with the organ. Others are fumbling with handkerchiefs. Brother Kevin is maneuvering his wheelchair down the aisle, legs useless as an orphan's, blood of Christ in his lap. He serves us from the tray of little cups, row by row, as Sister Kathy sings:

> *"See from his head, his hands, his feet,*
> *Sorrow and love flow mingled down..."*

And she's singing it not how I remember it, but low and hard and gritty like the blues:

> *"Did e'er such love and sorrow meet,*
> *Or thorns compose so rich a crown?"*

Sister Sterling is up out of the pew on her high heels now, waving her arms wildly above her silver hair and wide crimson hat. "So rich a crown!" she cries. "So rich a crown!"

> *"So rich a crown!" she cries.*
> *"So rich a crown!"*

I am playing peek-a-boo with Eva. Eva of last year's Marghita Hospital snapshots. Eva of the stick-thin arms; Eva of the Auschwitz face. Eva who might not make it. Eva who did make it, somehow, like a battered refugee—made it to a place, in Transylvania of all places, where love flows mingled down from gentle hands and feet.

"Peek!" Eva of the laughing eyes. "Boo!" Eva of the catch-me grin.

"Patty-cake, patty-cake, baker's man."

Eva of the nimble fingers, touching my face and beard, picking through my hair. Off with my glasses, on again, and back through my hair—strand by strand. She finds no lice, but there is love in these fingers, flowing like a stream, and I've fallen in.

I come up gasping, grabbing for broken bits of hope to keep me afloat. In the heavy current I find enough for a raft and haul myself up. I'm barely on. I'm okay, though—I'm thinking it might be better even than I can see, and I'm waving my arms in the air.

I'm riding a horse-drawn wagon. It is a Gypsy wagon, covered Conestoga-style, driven by a burly-armed man in black. Melanie huddles next to me, with her shoulders draped in a shawl and her toothless face tied up in a scarf. The kids are roughhousing in the back. Someone is leaning out of a van taking our picture, and I holler at the kids to sit up and wave. Dodging past us with great, long strides are the olive-skinned women, a green blur of smocks and hair flowing loose in the wind.

I am riding a rusted, old electric tram, lurching clackety-clack past rows of concrete apartment blocks, hanging on to the leather strap overhead. "Excuse me," I say. I wonder if the man knows English? I lift my carry-on into the overhead compartment. I settle into my seat, fasten the belt, and reach for the in-flight magazine. "Seven-Up, please, with ice." Down the runway we race and lift into the air. Out the window, where clouds should be, is a face. It is peering from behind metal bars and chain link wire, bruised. Its eyes are like fire.

I am riding a killer whale, holding on by the dorsal fin for life itself. Swiftly it swims, this great, black-skinned beast, harpooned and bleeding from the side. Twenty miles an hour, maybe thirty, and with a thrust of the tail, faster. I dig my fingernails into the fin flesh; I won't let go.

No, I won't let go now.

19

New Hope for Troubled Times

The LORD also will be a stronghold for the oppressed,
A stronghold in times of trouble.

Psalm 9:9 NASB

On a sweltering July day in 1992 the temperature in the room reached one hundred plus degrees. The staff of the State orphanage for three hundred boys and girls between the ages of six and sixteen sat before me as I lectured. My subject was "Mothering the Unmothered." My objective was to teach the workers the needs of abandoned children. Naively, I assumed that this information would encourage them to respond with a new motivation to care for the children in a loving manner. Yes, the orphans were a bunch of ragamuffin kids with runny noses and dirty clothes. Their heads were shaved because of lice, making it difficult to distinguish boys from girls. Still, I tried to make the point that these kids deserved to be valued and loved like our own birth children.

Some of the orphanage personnel dozed off while others skeptically folded their arms and glared at me. As I spoke, I wondered if any of my information was helpful. Abandoned children come with a great deal of emotional baggage. I had spent much of my adult life acquiring an understanding of their needs. Back home I had spent two decades raising my four adopted children. Although they were now grown, I had not forgotten the challenge of those years. How would I react working at minimal wage in an institution with hundreds of problem children. Maybe I, too, would be exhausted and doze off.

One staff person had charge of as many as fifty children.

Yet a few of the staff listened intently to what I had to say. I could easily tell which of them really cared for the orphans. I could see it in their eyes. As I spoke about the children, their lack of trust and how they misbehave because of their deeply felt pain, I saw a few tears.

After my seminar ended, several of the participants came and spoke to me through a translator. They explained that they wanted to help the orphans, but there were so many children and so few of them. Often one staff person had charge of as many as fifty children. They needed training to handle both the aggressive kids and the quiet, depressed ones. These men and women were from poor families themselves. Many faced stress in their own family life and were hurting folks.

> *As I spoke about the children,*
> *their lack of trust and how they misbehave*
> *because of their deeply felt pain,*
> *I saw a few tears.*

Fred and I came to Romania to help improve the quality of the orphans' lives. We quickly learned the problems would not be solved with a few seminars. As much as we tried, our approach in educating the staff would not unlock the caretakers' hearts and minds. Education was not enough to motivate the staff to care for abandoned Gypsy children. We felt overwhelmed by the enormity of a situation that seemed beyond change.

> *Education was not enough to motivate the staff*
> *to care for abandoned Gypsy children.*
> *We felt overwhelmed by the enormity of a situation*
> *that seemed beyond change.*

As we observed volunteers like Lars, Barbro, and their children, Sofia, David, and Par, modeling loving relationships with the older orphans, we began to see the problems in a different light. The orphanage staff and the children lacked mentors who would simply show them love and human kindness.

The orphanage staff and the children lacked mentors who would simply show them love and human kindness.

A Romanian friend said, "As a whole, Romania could be classified as a hopeless, depressed society." While I doubted this was a correct assessment, I did meet many discouraged Romanians.

One issue with the Romanian orphanage system is that most of the orphans have families. They are not orphans in the truest sense of the word. A large majority of abandoned children have parents living in a nearby village. Perhaps the father died and the mother remarried. The new husband may not want the child, and so he is placed in an orphanage. Extreme poverty is also a major factor. Another baby in the family means another mouth to feed, so the parents decide to allow the State to raise their child. We heard of one family that has nineteen children, and four of them are in the same orphanage. Another family cannot afford to heat their house in winter, so they decide to leave the new baby at the hospital. Some children are given to grandparents. They may be too old and feeble to care for them. This is the case with a set of twins abandoned at the hospital and eventually sent to Casa Alba.

A woman's wages were cut if she did not produce the required number of children by the time she was forty-five.

Under communism it was assumed that the State could do a better job at parenting the children than their parents. For twenty-four years, dictator Nicolae Ceausescu, who was executed in 1989, put pressure on women to have at least five children. A woman's wages were cut if she did not produce the required number of children by the time she was forty-five. The whole dynamic of the family was disrupted. Families had children they could not afford. Perhaps the father was out of a job or had a drinking problem. A foundation in Oradea discovered that 90 percent of the children in one orphanage had cases of alcoholism within their immediate families. A family has difficulty functioning under these circumstances.

Decades ago, many villagers placed their child in government-run boarding schools with the parents bringing the children home during summer vacations and holidays. Perhaps due to poverty, single motherhood, and alcoholism, more and more parents failed to return to take their children home. The boarding schools became year-round orphanages. Abandoned babies lived in the hospitals until they were three and then were moved to an orphanage for toddlers. After another three years, they were sent to an orphanage with a "special school" for the children.

Abandoned babies lived in the hospitals until they were three and then were moved to an orphanage for toddlers.

We know of some children who were severely traumatized before being abandoned. In one case, children witnessed their father murder their mother. The treatment in the orphanage further traumatized the children who received no help from their previous ordeal. Children who are clearly mentally ill are often given sedatives to control their behavior and keep them in a passive state. Some of these children sleep many hours of the day. I seldom saw them outside playing.

At night, Cadea's darkened halls were scary places.

Cadea was an orphanage for teens with the worst problems although there were exceptions like Imi and Zoli. Most of the boys had previously been labeled mentally limited. No special education teachers were available to help those with learning disabilities. At night, Cadea's darkened halls were scary places. Orphans moved in and out of whatever light was there. One evening, Fred spoke to a staff person on the night shift.

"Well, what do you do all night here?" Fred inquired.

"Oh, I am an artist and I paint," the man answered.

"Don't the children keep you from your painting?"

"No, they don't bother me. I just lock my door," the man said with a shrug. Apparently, he did not see the problem of allowing several hundred teenagers to roam the building at night with no supervision.

Afterward Fred remarked to me, "He is probably protecting himself from the kids by locking himself in."

Sadly, over the years, orphanages became businesses employing many local people. An orphanage might be located in a village where jobs are scarce. Workers can walk to their job and usually work with fellow villagers. With few other opportunities for work, many orphanage staff pay to get their jobs. When the orphanage population is reduced or the orphanage is closed, the villagers lose jobs and their income. The entire village suffers economically.

In the many years that I have been coming to Romania, I have observed that orphanage directors and assistants change positions frequently. As in any society, there are good directors as well as those who only see the position as a job.

Izidor Ruckel, a Romanian orphan adopted by a California family, in his book *Abandoned for Life* (St. Louis: JB Information Station, 2002), described the director of his orphanage in this way: "To tell you the truth, I think Viorel was the best director over all we'd had in the past. He checked our living conditions. Although Viorel had a drinking problem—you could smell the alcohol on his breath and the house nannies often gossiped about how he was often drunk on the job—and he chain-smoked cigarettes, he was still a good director for the children ... from an adult viewpoint. I can see how his frustrations at being unable to help us more, may have caused him to drink to dull those feelings."

Many of the children in an orphanage are mentally and emotionally handicapped, but some are normal in their abilities.

The dormitory and the school of an orphanage are run separately, and each has its own director. The school is under the authority of the Ministry of Education and is a school for handicapped children or "special school." Many of the children in an orphanage are mentally and emotionally handicapped, but some are normal in their abilities. A few very capable children may attend the normal school in the village alongside children from families. Children in the "special school" have handicap certificates that verify their need for this "special education." Sadly, many of these children are as capable as those attending the normal school, but they are denied opportunity for a good education.

Such labeling can be very unfair to children. In one instance, Fred took a child to be examined for entry into a regular school. After a ten-minute test, the psychologist said she had the intelligence of a severely mentally challenged child. I knew this was not so. Six months later, this girl has shown us that she can perform very well in a normal school. I asked myself, *What is the motivation for labeling these children as handicapped?*

Orphan culture is very complex.

A certain family feeling exists among the orphans. This connection and loyalty are very difficult for the casual visitor to see or understand. The children argue and fight and call each other "schmeck," which means jerk or geek. However, they hang together and look out for one another. Group connections may save some from the severe symptoms of attachment problems.

I would never steal from my friend.

The orphans may not have parents, but they are not alone. They have each other. Some lifelong friendships are formed in the orphanage. For some teens these relationships may be sexual, but many are purely friendships. The formation of such relationships is part of their determination to survive. I asked one teen orphan if he would protect his friend from a beating. He said no, because if a big guy was doing the hitting, then he would be beaten, too. However, he continued, "I would never steal from my friend." He understood that would be wrong.

Anything of value that a younger child had would not be secure in the orphanage. The practice of stealing from the weaker children is a game to many of the older orphans. Resisting might mean a fist in the face or a stick to the back. Occasionally, visiting foreigners bring gifts for the children. One group from Finland took five children on a weekend holiday. They gave the kids lots of nice clothes and even some money. I was told by one of the children that the gifts did not remain with the kids for long. The older kids stole and sold everything, possibly for food, cigarettes, or alcohol.

It is subtle, but the visitors have just furthered the children's expectations of future handouts.

Frequently, younger children are pressured to "butter up" the foreign visitors. This is how it goes. A visitor drives up to an orphanage and parks the car. Already some kids have spotted them. By some unseen grapevine, ten kids are quickly hanging on each visitor. Soon the visitors begin to dole out presents. They have made sure there are enough for all the kids. Hands reach for the western-made toy or electronic gadget. The visitors have just entered into collusion with the kids. They have "bought" friends. The kids "ooh and aah" over the gifts knowing that behind closed orphanage doors they will soon be taken by the older kids. It is subtle, but the visitors have just furthered the children's expectations of future handouts. Yes, there is some genuine interest and curiosity about the visitors. But, as one orphan told me, "They learn quickly to suck up to visitors, especially Americans."

Of course, the answer is to go with nothing but your offer of friendship. Yes, bring supplies and money, but give to a reliable organization working with the children. These people live and work in Romania and know what the kids really need.

Several years ago, I took a few children to the salon in Marghita to have their hair styled and highlighted. In the following weeks, many other children suddenly became very friendly and asked to go with me to Marghita to get their hair done. Considering their circumstances, this is not surprising. But I wanted to develop healthy relationships without the promises of goods and services. Since then, I have backed away from that practice and simply offer myself . . . a loving mother. Ultimately, this is what they really need.

> *I wanted to develop healthy relationships*
> *without the promises of goods and services.*

There are signs of progress in Romania's effort to improve the situation for its orphans. The number of children in orphanages has been reduced significantly, and many institutions have been closed. In 1990, after the revolution, it was estimated that there were 100,000 to 300,000 abandoned children in 500 orphanages. The exact figures are unknown. The official number is now reported to be about 30,000 children. These statistics sound encouraging, but they do not tell the whole story.

There are some basic reasons for the drop in the orphan count. Recent legislation prohibits any child under the age of two from moving to an institution. Of the several thousand babies abandoned each year in hospitals, some are being returned to their birth families, and foster families have been found for others. Yet some remain in hospitals for as long as two years. None of these babies are counted as orphans. After years of neglect and abuse in orphanages, many mentally limited young people live in institutions for the handicapped and are no longer included in the count of orphans. Some orphanages, with significant populations of children, are now called boarding schools. And many children who were "graduated" from orphanages when they turned eighteen now live on the streets. It is clear that at least some of Romania's abandoned children have simply been given new names.

Another sign of progress is the increase in those trained in psychology and social work. More people are now qualified to help the children, and they are making known the needs of Romania's abandoned children. Foster parents are being recruited to provide a family environment for institutionalized children. Some Romanian families are adopting younger children thereby saving them from years in an institution. Social workers are finding mothers who abandoned their children and evaluating family situations to determine if children can be reunited with their parents. The goal is to keep children with their birth families or to place them with foster or adoptive families. Because international adoptions are no longer possible, there is more pressure to find Romanian families for the children. We know every child needs a family.

FCE is only one of many organizations working in Romania to better the lives of orphans. However, more groups are needed to provide supportive living environments and to offer job training for the older children.

There is no adequate replacement for the support of caring family members who share a common bond.

Orphanages all over the world struggle with the same issues that have plagued Romanian orphanages…overcrowding, insufficient staff, corruption, abuse, problematic children. An orphanage is not a place of nurturing and healing for children. One of our adopted sons spent some of his early years in a Christian orphanage in the Philippines where he was beaten when he wet his bed. When caring for children is only a job, a worker remains emotionally distant. Add to this the multiple problem behaviors of large numbers of children, how can an orphanage take the place of raising a child in a loving family? Simply put, it cannot. There is no adequate replacement for the support of caring family members who share a common bond.

Jesus Christ is present in the orphanages to help the children through the really hard times.

Even with all the difficulties orphans and orphanage staff face I have seen many hopeful changes. The children are responding to the biblical truth that they are uniquely created by a God who loves them. Jesus Christ is present in the orphanages to help the children through the really hard times. This is more than a theory to them. It is a lifeline they cling to.

When I told one boy about the surgery that one of my children was facing, he said, "Well, let's pray right now." Everyone in the room stopped their chatter, and this boy prayed a heartfelt prayer for healing for my son.

Several years ago, there was a boy who I did not like to be around. He pretended he was a dog and tried to bite me. I would shoo him away, but he would return to sneak up on me. Recently, I was in a prayer group with him. He prayed intensely and fervently. After our group time, he went around and hugged each person. He enjoys going to the old folks' home and giving words of encouragement. He has become a loving, caring Christian young man. What an incredible blessing he is to all who know him.

Father, please give us wisdom to know how to help the children. Help us support the efforts of the Romanian officials to find better places for the children. Help us to find kind and loving adoptive and foster parents for the children.

20

Silently . . . Like Death

The stories we tell, and the stories we don't tell,
shape our pasts and define our lives.
PBS Adoption: A Gathering, 1998-1999

A frightening twist came to light in our ministry to orphans. As the children's trust in us grew, they began to tell us their stories . . . heartbreaking tales.

"My family lives down the road. They kept five children, but they gave me away." Then, silence . . . and the unspoken question, *Why did they give me away?*

Tales of mistreatment by the orphanage staff and older teens began to emerge. At first the children only spoke of physical cruelty, but as their trust grew, stories of sexual exploitation unfolded.

A few orphans who are out of the system are willing to tell the real stories of their orphanage experiences. One such young man is Izidor Ruckel. In spite of a deformed leg, he was able to overcome his handicap to become a champion swimmer at Temecula Valley High School in California. His orphanage experiences in the early nineties remain vivid in his memory, and he writes about one unforgettable episode in his book, *Abandoned for Life* (St. Louis: JB Information Station, 2002, p 48).

> Silently, like Death, she walked into another room and returned with the thick oak broomstick. Silently, she strode toward my bed and I began to truly fear for my life. Completely out of control again, she angrily tore off my tattered blanket, raised the broomstick over her head and beat me

almost senseless. It hurt me so bad I thought she had broken many of my bones, surely a rib or two. After she was done with my beating, she turned and started beating Chobbie until she had no more strength left to wield her weapon. Then she left as silently as she had come . . . like Death!

Now a young adult, Izidor is telling the world that not only were Romanian orphans neglected in the orphanage, they also suffered physical maltreatment.

Fortunately, Izidor was befriended by a kind woman who took him into her home on weekends. Perhaps he survived because of this caring person.

Orphanage staff and orphans join in a conspiracy of silence.

It may sound strange to hear that orphanage staff and orphans join in a conspiracy of silence, but the orphans have observed the consequences of "telling" and they are afraid. More beatings might come and life will be hell . . . for those who whisper the truth. One younger teenager said he was beaten with a tire iron. Rarely are the victims of such incidents photographed because for the last decade cameras are not allowed in the orphanages. However, volunteers who have observed children the day after a beating report that they have seen wounds and bruises.

The expose' of the appalling conditions suffered by Romania's orphans that appeared on western television in 1990 flung open orphanage doors for the world to see. And what we saw stunned us. Starving and severely neglected children languished in dilapidated institutions hidden away in villages in the Romanian countryside. Many may wonder what progress has been made in the years since the media first broke the story.

The September 24, 2006, edition of the *Sunday Times UK*, Timesonline.com, reports:

> In a series of interviews with *The Sunday Times*, Romanian ministers, orphanage directors and other officials all acknowledged serious failings in the country's childcare system more than 16 years after appalling conditions were discovered during the collapse of communism. While progress has been made to meet demands from Brussels for EU entry— such as the closure of large state-run orphanages—many problems remain, including the care of handicapped and abandoned children.

There are people who truly care about the orphans. However, good workers are intimidated, and they rarely report mistreatment of the children out of fear of losing their jobs. Unemployment is high in Romania, and finding a good job is difficult. Few will risk losing their job to protect a Gypsy orphan.

I am especially close to one boy from a state-run institution. I will call him Andre. One evening as I was talking with Andre, he began to tell me "secrets" from his past. His words seemed to flow from a need to release the deep heartache within.

Andre was eight when he was moved to his second orphanage. The first thing he learned was that older boys beat the little kids at night. At times, the staff would pay the older boys to harass the younger children. Andre soon learned to sleep with a mattress over him and with his head facing the wall.

Andre soon learned to sleep with a mattress over him and with his head facing the wall.

"I couldn't put the mattress over my head because I had to breathe. Going to bed and waking up were the scariest time. I never knew when one of the boys would come in and hit me. I had bruises and places where my skin puffed up from being hit so much."

"How could you even go to sleep?" I asked.

"Sometimes I was afraid to sleep. They beat all the younger boys and girls. We all cried and screamed. When we made noise, they beat us harder. No one came to help us."

Everyone knew, but everyone remained silent.

Why would the caretakers want the children beaten at night? Was this to keep them in line? Was it some kind of perverted pleasure in hearing children crying? Was it to break their will and make them do things they did not want to do?

When I asked Andre why the children were beaten, he shrugged his shoulders and said, "*Nu stiu.* I do not know."

Andre interrupted my thoughts and added, "We had to massage a teacher."

"You what?"

"We had to massage her back, arms, and legs."

"She made you do this?"

"Yes, yes. And we had to pull out the hairs on her legs."

Astonished again, I asked, "You what?"

"You know, with those pincher things."

"You must mean tweezers."

Andre giggled and nodded his head. "Yes."

I heaved a sigh and said, "I am sorry. Children should not be treated like that."

"I was just a little boy. There were so many children. I had a difficult time finding my room. I was afraid all the time. Sometimes the teachers hit my fingers. See, you can see the places on my fingers and nails where I was hit with stick."

I look. One finger looks like there could be some nerve damage. I think, *No wonder many of the orphans are emotionally disturbed.*

I am in shock. With my head in my hands, I weep for this wonderful boy who faced such humiliation. An orphan's secrets are not easy to hear. Yet perhaps it is best to know the truth so that when an orphan behaves inappropriately we will understand the pervasive anguish in his heart.

An orphan's secrets are not easy to hear.

Other stories were told. One of a staff person who had a nail in the toe of his shoe and kicked the children. All types of instruments for punishment were used . . . broom handles, cords, belts, a strip of metal, a tree branch laced with salt, a fist. A unique form of punishment was devised by a teacher who made the children kneel down, and then with a running jump, he would give them a karate kick.

Another teen told me his story. Suddenly I understood why he is so fearful, yet desperate for attention. He was beaten along with others, but he suffered something even worse. He was used sexually by the big boys. He is nervous . . . as if he cannot rest. My young friend had no place where he felt safe, not in bed and certainly not in the boys' bathroom. He never completely undresses, not even in the shower, for fear of being assaulted. Older boys intimidated and humiliated him. One older boy used my friend's toothbrush to clean his shoes.

Fred witnessed a staff person scream at him for getting a mark on a wall. When he was making a birthday card for Fred, he accidentally bumped the wall with a paintbrush. As he was on his knees scrubbing the wall, this woman berated him with a tirade of foul verbiage. I wonder how long it will take to bring healing to this teen's heart.

I wonder how long it will take to bring healing to this teen's heart.

Girls were not exempt from various forms of punishment. Two young girls were told to remove their clothes in front of a group of boys before they were whipped. Sexual harassment is a common occurrence. Girls told of older boys and male staff grabbing their breasts and of being sexually molested. One teen reported that her assailant threatened to poke her eyes out with a piece of glass if she told.

Sometimes male staff were assigned to the girls' dormitory. Frequently they would "accidentally" walk in on teenage girls when they were undressing. Few girls escaped being molested. Forever etched in their memories are scenes of their degradation.

I wonder if this ill-treatment is a local problem or pervasive in all of Romania's orphanages. From the reports of children, volunteers, and workers in nongovernment organizations, it appears to be widespread. I corresponded with an American doctor who has worked extensively in Romania and has adopted Romanian children. He told me that abuse is throughout the orphanage system. He was reluctant to allow me to use his name in this book.

The orphanages were a living nightmare.

> The most defining thing about me is that for eighteen years I was an orphan of the state. Everyone in the world has heard about Romanian orphans. The orphanages were a living nightmare. We were starved, beaten, and sexually abused on various occasions. We were treated worse than animals. The conditions were so bad...unimaginable.
>
> I remember we were some of the little kids who were abused sexually. Many nights we slept hungry.
>
> When I was little, I was beaten so much because I was a child who always cried. If the staff saw you crying, you were beaten until you stopped.

After this bright young man earned some academic awards in school, he thought he could go to officials and speak out. They listened and then labeled him as "crazy" and sent him to a psychiatric ward for three months. When he returned to the orphanage he said, "Life went on as though nothing had happened."

Again, everyone knew, but everyone remained silent.

Sex trafficking is no secret in Eastern European countries.

Sex trafficking is no secret in Eastern European countries. In his book, *The Natashas: Inside the New Global Sex Trade* (New York: Arcade Publishing, 2004, pp 14-15), Victor Malarek asserts: "And in Romania, many orphanages are complicit in letting girls fall victim to trafficking networks."

When a young woman "graduates" from an institution, she is turned out on the streets. There are few government safety nets for these young women. Nongovernment organizations in Romania attempt to pick up the slack in teaching skills and offering jobs. Yet much more needs to be done to alleviate this immense social problem.

I wonder if any of the children I know might be vulnerable to sex traffickers. I do know of a case involving an orphanage employee who arranged sex with one of the girls for the payment of a few dollars. I can only hope that this was an infrequent incident.

Although most officials really care about the children, change comes slowly. Many people need a new mind-set toward orphans and Gypsies.

With Romania's entry into the European Union, efforts are underway to raise standards of care for the orphans. In the future, I hope all reports of child abuse will be taken seriously. Orphan behavior is often very frustrating to caregivers, and they need to be trained in safe behavior management techniques. There are acceptable methods to restrain an out-of-control child. Discipline can involve more than physical punishment. Caring for a group of problematic children is a very difficult job, and we must pray for the caregivers we know.

As I mull over what my responsibility is before God, I think, *I cannot remain passive or remain silent. Why don't other caring people do something about the ill-treatment of orphans? Who will advocate for the orphans if Christians don't?*

More pointedly, I ask myself . . .

How can I protect the children
from those who would seek to prey
on the weakest in our society?
How many in harm's way can be rescued?

21

Broken Wings

I said, "God I hurt."
And God said, "I know."
I said, "God, I cry a lot."
And God said,
"That is why I gave you tears."
Anonymous

†the boy appeared to be mentally limited. He lived in a state orphanage for teen boys. Somehow, in his mind he believed his job was to push the wheeheelbarrow around and to sweep up fallen leaves. He didn't realize that as soon as he picked up the leaves more would fall. When there were no leaves, he spent hours pushing the empty wheelbarrow around the paved courtyard.

The boy found a treasure
in a pile of leaves . . . a baby bird.

On the day of our visit, the boy found a treasure in a pile of leaves . . . a baby bird. I held my breath wondering if he would squeeze the life out of the small creature. Yet he was quite gentle. He held it up very carefully to show the other boys. Then he threw it up in the air to see if it would fly away. The bird fluttered to the ground. Surely it would die if left on the ground. I thought he might take it to his room to care for it.

As we continued to watch, the boy did something amazing. Carefully, he lifted the bird and placed it on the roof of a nearby shed. For a few minutes, he stood looking at the bird, and then he returned to his wheelbarrow to continue with his "work." Somehow this boy knew that the little bird needed its mother. Its only chance for survival was for its mother to come back to care for it.

Oh, that this boy and the others living behind the high walls of the orphanage would be rescued! These boys are our friends. FCE's volunteers have known many of them since they were little boys at another orphanage in a village about an hour away. After their eighth year of school, they were sent to this soul-less place for high school. After this, maybe they will get a job making shoelaces in a factory.

Fred and I visited with Farkas, Gyuri, Cipri, Mihai, Sorin, and Florin. A friendly staff person chatted with us. He said he has worked here in the dormitory for eight years. He hoped to have some sports activities for the boys sometime. I wondered if that would happen.

The only place they had to play
was outside in a bare concrete courtyard
cluttered with piles of rubble
and surrounded by high cement walls.

The only place they had to play was outside in a bare concrete courtyard cluttered with piles of rubble and surrounded by high cement walls. In the center was a basketball hoop, net missing. There were no balls to play with. *All these teenage boys . . . with television as their only activity,* I thought. *Will they ever be able to function normally in Romanian society?*

With heavy hearts, we hugged them and said good-bye. Large metal doors closed with a bang behind us, and we walked out to the street. From the outside no one would know about the "broken wings" waiting to be set free.

At the age of seventeen, **Daniel** *was an angry, disagreeable boy.*
He lived in Cadea for three years. Daniel was disrespectful to the volunteers and stole whatever he could. Many times he was able to gain temporary freedom by running away from Cadea.

Barbro and the other volunteers invited the boys to a camp in the mountains. During a time of prayer, Daniel's heart softened, and he asked the others to pray for him. The day after camp ended, he went to church and heard the pastor speak about a personal relationship with Jesus that He offered to anyone who asked. The next night, the volunteers joined with the boys at Cadea for a time of worship. Phyllis Parker knew the boys quite well and spoke very seriously to them. As Phyllis looked at each boy she said, "You do not know how many days you have left on this earth." That evening Daniel accepted Jesus as his Lord and Savior. His spiritual awakening occurred over a period of three days.

The following day, the Cadea staff took a group of orphans to Oradea for an outing. Daniel left the group and joined a gang of street children. They were hanging out along the River Crisul that runs swiftly through Oradea. It was an extremely hot day, and a few teens decided to cool off in the river. Daniel bragged to his friends that he was a good swimmer. To prove it, he jumped into the river. His bluff quickly turned into tragedy. As Daniel reached for a floating plastic bottle, he suddenly disappeared beneath the surface of the muddy water. The strong current carried him away.

Barbro did not know whether Daniel was alive or dead until his body was discovered a week later. One of the street kids called Florin Costea in Marghita. Florin was asked to identify the body to make sure it was Daniel. Florin walked down to the riverbank near a bridge where Daniel's bloated body was discovered. Yes, it was Daniel. Rumors spread that the boy was depressed and committed suicide. Yet Barbro and others who knew him well were emphatic that this was not so. Just the day before he had accepted Jesus as his Savior and rejoiced in his new faith.

David lived all of his life in institutions,

and his emotional scars went very deep. His story reminded me of the bird in the orphanage courtyard. He flapped his wings but flew nowhere. Barbro tried to help him learn to fly again. He was given several jobs, including one at Casa Alba, but he didn't keep them. When he failed, he would come to Barbro saying, "Just give me one more chance and I will work hard." He failed time after time. He just couldn't make it.

Tragically David decided to live life his own way, and he chose a very destructive path. One evening, he went to a nearby city and began drinking in a bar with his buddies. They watched as a man they knew opened his wallet at the bar. The boys looked at each other with knowing looks. This man had a lot of money and expensive things in his apartment. When he turned to leave, they followed him out of the bar.

David could have stopped here, but he didn't. The man was drunk, and they followed him to his apartment. Since the man knew the boys, in his drunken stupor he invited them in. They began to demand his money and started to beat him. In the ensuing struggle, the man collapsed and died.

The boys stole his money and took many things from his apartment. Later, the police found the boys and arrested them. David steadfastly maintained his innocence. One of the boys told the police that David did not hit the man, but he was jailed anyway.

Months dragged into years without a trial. Every week Barbro faithfully went to visit him. Sometimes the jailers would not let her see him. When they did, he was not allowed to talk about the crime. Finally, David was tried, convicted, and sentenced to twenty-five years in prison. I often think of this very handsome young man. I have not seen him since he went to prison.

David left a girlfriend and a baby behind. The baby will be grown before David gets out of prison. The last time Barbro visited him, he said, "I realize now that I hated myself and wanted to be away from everyone. I live in prison and I got what I thought I wanted. I was too proud."

During his years of confinement, his heart has softened. He asked Barbro for a Bible so he can read the words of God. David is an orphan who has gone from one prison to another. We pray that behind the steel doors he will find freedom from the prison keeping his soul in bondage all these years.

The LORD sets the prisoners free.
The LORD opens the eyes of the blind;
The LORD raises up those who are bowed down.
Psalm 146:7–8 NASB

A Scrap of Paper
by Mary Dewey

My granddaughter, Mary, was eleven when she first traveled to Romania. She has returned every summer and several times in the winter. In the following story Mary describes an orphan who struggles to believe she is of value to anyone.

This winter I got to spend time at an orphanage with a girl named Florica. I don't know her as well as some of the other kids because she moved to her present orphanage from another orphanage last year. She is a beautiful girl, with dark, curly hair and a smile that fills up her whole face. But when she describes herself, she says only one thing: I'm crazy. She doesn't mean fun or playful or adventurous; she means mentally ill. The other kids tell me about her fits, when she screams uncontrollably and lashes out at anyone trying to help. She tells me about the pills she takes to make her normal. I wonder if anyone can be normal in an orphanage like this.

One day my friend, Sarah, and I were sitting in a room with Florica and some other kids when Florica pulled out a pen and a scrap of paper. She handed it to Sarah and asked her to write something on it—anything she wanted. Sarah wrote three sentences in Romanian and handed it back to her.

"You are beautiful. You are special. You are loved."

Less then ten minutes later the paper had been grabbed by other kids, scribbled on, and ripped until it was unrecognizable. Personal possessions, even scraps of paper, don't last long at this orphanage. But I knew that Florica would remember those words. I also knew that she didn't believe them. My hope is that someday, if we tell her those words over and over, if we show them to her again and again, she will finally know that they are true.

Cool Water
by Melanie Dewey

Melanie, my daughter-in-law, first visited Romania with Fred and me in 1997. She joined the Loving Arms team in 2005 and experienced her first week of camp with the orphans. That week had a long-lasting effect on her heart.

How do you become a human being when you've never been treated like one? How do you love when you've never been given any love to pass on to another? Orphans are little kids, big kids, obnoxious kids, babies wrapped in white cloths, and the ones whose mothers say they'll come back for them someday. Is it any wonder the older children behave in strange ways?

Some of the big kids—teenagers—still sit on the floor doing the "orphan rock." Forward and back, forward and back. They learn to do this as babies—stimulating themselves when there is no one to touch them.

These children are born to a cursed world, handed back by the arms that first cradled them. Did their mothers hold them even once? This world has had nothing to give them, only something to take. Abandoned children with their souls ripped apart lie in white cages passing for cribs—the peeling metal bars the limits of their world.

No brown eyes gaze into theirs. Their little minds try to understand the river of sensations . . . try to find a smile in the motionless room . . . try to hear a "Mama" in the burble of noises . . . try to make some connection . . . and finally, don't try at all. The river becomes a trickle, then dries up. The bars, once painted white, chip away and turn to rust.

Now in a cage called an orphanage, the bars have grown into their own bodies and minds. We meet an official who considers himself an important director, but he only directs the cages around the children's hearts. But the wells are so deep and dry. The river sinks into the desert and disappears. Still no river, and all so thirsty.

"Who has water? Do you know where I can find some water? Please, I have not had a cold drink for such a very long time."

Into this cage step two Swedish young women, Louise and Linda. Their hearts are bleeding and broken—bleeding a river of water. The river of life flows clear and strong, sweeping children in its flood.

Oh, God, pour down Your cool healing rain. Make this small, small cup pressed against chapped lips a flood of water for those failing of thirst in this dry land.

teaching them to fly

**Karyn Dewey Mitchell with Lavinia
and Camelia at Casa Alba**

**Josif & Loving Arms
team member Mark Mason**

***B**aby at Casa Alba & Loving Arms
team member, James Rowe*

Florin Costea and orphans

22

Camp's Here

The LORD's lovingkindnesses indeed never cease,
For His compassions never fail.
They are new every morning; Great is Your faithfulness.

Lamentations 3:22-23 NASB

The idea of a week at camp came from Florin Costea. He wanted the children to have an outdoor experience, and a rustic resort with hot mineral springs in the tiny village of Chislaz seemed like a good place for the first camp. This would be the first ever camp for these orphans. With their clothes thrown into duffel bags, the rough and tumble boys of Cadea were packed into vans and hauled off to camp. Florin and the boys unloaded the vans, set up their army surplus tents, and built a campfire. They were delighted to cook their own food over the open fire. For swimming, there was a four-foot deep hot water pool which looked less than inviting to me.

Given the freedom to simply have fun at the camp, the boys went wild. Teens who had never been free for an entire week for sports and swimming romped, yelled, splashed, and punched each other. Our two teenage daughters, Wendi and Christine, taught the boys how to play volleyball, and they all had a great time.

We were not prepared, however, for the negative reaction of the other vacationers who did not want to share their holiday with a bunch of orphans. The boys were not socialized, and they did not know how to act around people. When contacted the following year, the owner of Chislaz did not want the orphans to come back. He had too many complaints from other guests about the rowdy boys. The foundation needed to find another place to hold a camp for the orphans.

One place came to mind . . . Padurea Neagra or the Black Forest of Transylvania. In the foothills south of Marghita is a beautiful dark forest. This quiet world of nearly impenetrable forest is a sharp contrast to the children's raucous and chaotic environment in the gray concrete buildings of their orphanage.

There was one huge obstacle to overcome.

There was one huge obstacle to overcome. The concrete two-story camp building, owned by Marghita Hospital and once used for staff vacations, had not been used for years and was in a state of disrepair. Windows were broken, the roof leaked, and rubbish littered the building and grounds. Lars and Florin organized a group of boys to haul out the trash and prepare to paint. Loose paint was scraped from wood windows, and several boys began the tedious job of painting windows and walls.

The boys literally immersed themselves in their work, and several dark heads of hair became white or green with paint. New red tiles replaced the old leaking roof. The boys lived at the camp during the time they worked at renovating the building. They were very pleased to be included on the construction team, and when we complimented them for their work, the smiles on their faces expressed their appreciation. We were proud of them for their hard work to prepare the camp for the future.

The boys literally immersed themselves in their work, and several dark heads of hair became white or green with paint.

There was a big push to get the camp ready for the first group of campers. Days before the camp opened, trash was piled outside the building fifteen feet high. I could not imagine how it could all be hauled away in time, but it was.

The building looked great with the dormitory furnished with new bunk beds. Each bed had a small cabinet next to it for personal items. The cafeteria sparkled with a fresh coat of paint and bright curtains over the windows. The kitchen was equipped with commercial appliances donated from Sweden, including a dishwasher. On the upper floor, there was a large room called "the club." This room was for general meetings and worship gatherings.

Their much anticipated week of camp was finally here— a precious time of freedom from the institution which offered little more than day-to-day drudgery

Finally, the building was ready for the first day of camp. A van full of teenagers arrived from the nearby orphanage. The doors were thrown open, and the van coughed up its load of children amid cheers and shouts. Their much anticipated week of camp was finally here—a precious time of freedom from the institution which offered little more than day-to-day drudgery. Most of all, it was a time of growing friendships with caring folks from Sweden, Germany, California, and Colorado who volunteered to staff one or two weeks of camp.

*After a half dozen years of "doing camp," our son, Scott,
reflects on the first year (2000) he brought a team to Padurea Neagra:*

Our first day appeared to be pretty much a disaster. The orphans, coming from a bleak place where they are malnourished, neglected, beaten, and bored, arrived in such a frenzy of excitement that they could barely be controlled. We had been told that the children were developmentally delayed and very immature for their ages, and this was certainly evident by the chaos at hand. The orphanage staff was no help, retiring to the shade of a tree and ignoring us. We managed a few activities but ended the day deeply discouraged. We did hold a meeting with the orphanage staff. They were rather scornful of our team, but we did come up with a working agreement as to our respective roles, and they agreed to help manage the children the following day.

> *The orphans, coming from a bleak place where
> they are malnourished, neglected, beaten, and bored,
> arrived in such a frenzy of excitement
> that they could barely be controlled.*

The difficulties of that first day made the following days seem all the more remarkable. The children, divided into four groups with team colors and mascots, became very attached to their team leaders and the rest of our group including the teen translators. They participated enthusiastically in our activities and took great pride in Bible memory and understanding the symbolism of their "salvation bracelets." While still pretty wild much of the time, they made efforts to please and go with the program.

We gave awards and keepsakes each day. As they had virtually no personal possessions at all, even the simplest items such as balloons or Polaroid snapshots became treasures.

Even more amazing was the transformation we saw among the orphanage staff. Slowly over the week they warmed up to us and even participated in the worship sessions. By the end of the week they were shedding tears at saying good-bye and exchanging addresses. Our own attitudes softened as well—our anger at how they have treated these children gave way to some measure of appreciation of the incredible challenges they face every day of the year.

**Pastor Ken Roberts
Loving Arms team 2000
with orphan boys at Camp Joy**

Each year following camp the Loving Arms team writes letters to the children during the year, and the children respond with their letters. Here are some of the messages they wrote to our family.

"Chris. I am so glad you took care of me when I was crying. I love you with all my heart."

"My dear friend, Benny, I had fun with you in the evening program at the Black Forest. I love you so much with all my heart and soul. Thank you for the pictures that you showed us at camp. Benny, I will cry for you all the time."

Dear Melanie, your heart is so beautiful. Please don't forget me and I will never forget you. Never! I am so glad you helped me at camp."

"Dear Mary, I love you very much and you are so important to me. I am so glad that you were in the purple group with me. I hope that you come back next year, because you are my sister. I kiss. I love you.

"Dear Scott, I want you to know that I miss you a lot and can't wait until next summer so we can have more good times together and talk more."

"To Mary, please say 'hi' to your whole family, and that I miss you all. I can't wait until you all can come next summer. I don't know what to do without you. I can't wait to see you again. I love you very much. I am doing just okay. But I am learning English with Karleen and Fred. Now I know a lot, but not a huge amount. I am not perfect."

"Dear Chris, you became my friend. We drew together at camp. You draw very beautifully. I will miss your hugs, your smile, and your friendship."

Dear Melanie, I'm so glad you were in my group. I know that I am in your heart. You know that you are like a mother for me. Thank you for helping with tampons. I miss you. It hurt so bad when you left us. The green group says, 'hi.' And they are thinking of you and praying for your family. I like your family's smiles. Don't forget that God is with you and your whole family. You have such a wonderful family, smiling and having fun. I cry for you. I tink of you and I will love you until i die. I love your hugs. To the whole family, I love you."

Over the years the orphans have flooded the Loving Arms team with notes and letters. It seems incredible to me that children who have survived so long without being loved can pour out love from their hearts. Perhaps of greatest value at camp is the love the team showers upon each camper. Although some children come with hearts hardened by years of rejection, in the safe and loving camp environment they slowly begin to soften. We are thankful to God that the children give us their trust and love us back in such awesome ways.

We are thankful to God that the children give us their trust and love us back in such awesome ways.

Tika and Zoli

A new Loving Arms team is formed in October each year.

A new Loving Arms team is formed in October each year. The team meets every other week to plan the camp program, to study Romanian, and to write support letters to raise funds needed for travel and camp expenses. Donated athletic shoes, socks, and T-shirts are collected for the children. In February, the team gathers for a weekend retreat in the mountains of Colorado to "live out" the theme for that summer's camp. Through prayer and group exercises, the team works through the camp theme, deepening each person's understanding of the biblical truth to be offered to the children.

The spiritual journey for the team begins long before the first day of camp. The team works through the camp theme, deepening each person's understanding the biblical truth to be offered to the children.

In 2003, I joined the Loving Arms camp team. Although usually I am involved with the babies in the hospital and the children in Casa Alba, I wanted to have a "camp experience" with the orphans. We traveled to Romania in June by way of Budapest, Hungary. It took four hours to drive from Budapest to the Romanian border and another two hours to reach the camp. It was a beautiful, sunny day when we arrived at camp in the Black Forest. The bright, blue sky with white, puffy clouds lifted my spirits. Romanian music drifted in and out from a neighboring cottage.

Upon arrival, we moved our baggage and more than twenty large boxes into the building. The guys got settled in their bunkroom, and the women and girls in another. Then the team got to work getting organized for the first day of camp. It seemed like Christmas as our young team members opened the boxes of camp supplies—shoes, socks, T-shirts, sports supplies, make-up, and craft supplies of all sorts.

> ### *The Loving Arms team was prepared to give the orphans from a nearby village an unforgettable "camp experience."*

"Here's the green craft box."

"Who has the supply list?"

"Where are the diapers for Casa Alba?"

"Which box has the basketballs?"

"Is this the make-up for the girls?"

The Loving Arms team was prepared to give the orphans from a nearby village an unforgettable "camp experience." The day after we arrived we received some unsettling news. Instead of a group of younger children, the children coming to camp would be a mix of ages from ten to seventeen. We asked questions of each other.

> ### *Instead of a group of younger children, the children coming to camp would be a mix of ages from ten to seventeen.*

"Will we have enough large size shoes?"

"What will we do with the problem kids? Do we send them back to the orphanage where they might be beaten?"

"Will the older kids abuse the younger ones in the dormitory at night?"

"Should we separate an older girl from the younger girls who are afraid of her? Can we break through her tough exterior and get to her heart?"

"Do we have enough adults to control the kids?"

On Monday morning, with mixed feelings, a group of us stood outside the camp building and waited for the orphans. We were told there would be some tough girls and boys in this group. A few on our team were anxious about the week ahead. One young woman felt totally overwhelmed. Perhaps the Casa Alba baby team would have been a better place for her. Jeanine, who had coordinated the crafts and the curriculum planning, realized some of what we planned wouldn't work well with the older teens. Weeks of preparation . . . so many good ideas . . . Now they had to be scrapped or radically changed to fit this age group.

The team had prepared all year for this day. We struggled to be flexible as we scrambled to change our plans. We prayed that morning that God would use us in our weakness. We felt so inadequate, but we chose to trust God to be our strength and to work in the hearts of the children.

> *We prayed that morning that God*
> *would use us in our weakness.*
> *We felt so inadequate,*
> *but we chose to trust God to be our strength*
> *and to work in the hearts of the children.*

The children arrived excited and shouting for joy. They were shown their dorm rooms . . . one for boys and one for girls. After the children settled on which person would sleep in what bed, they were directed to the "club" room upstairs for a group meeting. The camp rules for the week were announced. "Everyone must have fun."

The camp rules for the week were announced.

"Everyone must have fun."

Another "rule" brought cheers. "You can eat all you want."

A camp schedule was posted. Breakfast at 8:00, general meeting at 9:00, and then groups at 9:45. The children were divided into groups of seven or eight campers. Each group had their special color and was given green, red, blue, or yellow T-shirts. One of the first projects was to decorate the shirts with puffy paints. Often the children painted the name of their group on their T-shirts and the names of those in the group. As they lined up before mealtime, the group leaders would call out the group names. "Grupa verde." "Grupa rosu." "Grupa galben." "Grupa albastru." The camp leader chose the group with the straightest line to enter first.

Group time focused on a Bible lesson and discussion. Each group had a leader, assistant, and a translator. Some of the experienced, younger team members have learned to speak Romanian, but for those with less language ability, it is amazing how much can be communicated with a few phrases, smiles, laughter, and affection.

> *It is amazing how much an be communicated*
> *with a few phrases, smiles, laughter, and affection.*

Craft time was after lunch, followed by free time and swimming by groups in the small waist-deep pool. Other free-time activities included basketball, time on the swings, and water balloon fights. Some children liked to go for walks or just sit and talk. Many close friendships were formed with the team members. Tug of war was a favorite game. Groups challenged each other, Grupa verde against Grupa rosu. The Romanians pulled against the Loving Arms team and volunteers and girls against boys. At 3:30 there was a snack of fruit or cookies.

At 4:30, everyone met for an hour of fun—hilarious skits and humorous songs. The camp cookout Thursday evening was a great time for all with hot dogs cooked over an open fire, chips and s'mores—roasted marshmallows and chocolate sandwiched between graham crackers. I remember that some of the orphanage staff had never seen marshmallows. We showed them how to roast the marshmallows on a stick. At first they were hesitant but then saw that it was great fun.

After supper we gathered in the "club" for the evening meeting and worship hour. The children really enjoyed the evening program. My grandson, Ben, and his friend, Kalen, were the camp photographers. Each night they projected photos of the day's activities on the wall. It was wonderful to see the excitement on the campers' faces as their pictures were shown. The whole room was filled with laughter.

Then the mood of the evening changed as we sang worship and praise songs. A few of the young translators were part of the worship team. Several of the teens joined them in leading the singing. The children love to sing, and the choruses filled the room.

Then the mood of the evening changed as we sang worship and praise songs.

Then the mood of the evening changed as we sang worship and praise songs. A few of the young translators were part of the worship team. Several of the teens joined them in leading the singing. The children love to sing, and the choruses filled the room.

One evening, Imi, a young man who grew up in orphanages, told his story of survival and faith. Last of all, we took prayer requests from the children. One boy wanted us to pray that the children would not be beaten so much. Hands were laid on different children as the group prayed for them. We cried with the children and hugged each other during those precious moments.

Then the day was over and it was time for bed. A few of the teens stayed up to talk to team members. We were tired, but it was good to have a day with children who needed our love.

After the evening program the team met for a debriefing time. Several who at first felt overwhelmed by the children were feeling much more confident. For others, their emotions were overpowering and tears rolled down their cheeks as they spoke of the day's experiences. The children's stories were shocking. Some were withdrawn and mentally disturbed. Those of us who knew the children from previous camps were so happy to be with them again. Sadly, the week went by too fast for all of us.

There is almost no end to amazing camp stories.

Scott tells about Olympia, a girl with limited capacities, who generally does not talk at all. During a recent camp, as Scott was pushing her on a swing, she began to sing a little song. Scott was stunned—this was a song he made up and sang to her *four years before!* After four years, she remembered!

An older boy, Ghita, suffered a serious head injury during a game at camp and spent several days in a hospital. He felt the prayers and love of the entire team. In a miraculous way, his wounds healed with no lasting impairment.

We saw other children, who refused to go in the pool, finally overcome their fear and excitedly splash and shout and laugh with others. Of course, some team members were thrown in the pool with them.

Two members of our team, Diane Pulvermiller and Barb Demolar, traveled to Romania to see the children during the Christmas and New Year's holidays in 2004. Diane, a fiery and compassionate redhead, had decided to assume leadership of the Loving Arms team that year. She is deeply committed to the orphans. With other team members, she has continued winter visits to Marghita to see the children.

Diane says, "There is a sense that we have been in a holy place and shared God's holy work. I don't say that lightly. While I found Romania as a whole to be beautiful and hospitable, the orphanages are . . . capable of sucking all shreds of dignity from a child. We could show you pictures, but you wouldn't know. You wouldn't know until you hold the children and feel their tight, guarded bodies. You wouldn't know until you hear the fear in their voices and see the bleakness in their eyes. You wouldn't know until you see them abuse each other as they have been abused. And unless you know that darkness, you cannot know what a miracle—miracle!—it was, by the end of our time together at summer camp, to hear their prayers and their singing and their laughter."

Each team member and each child leaves camp with memories of hilarious times together but also with a deepening desire to more fully know God. His presence is felt at camp in a powerful way. As one team member said, "There are not enough words to describe what happened this week."

Scott says:

I came home more drained than ever after the two-week trip last summer. To be honest, I wondered if I would be up for doing Romania again this year. I told my wife, Melanie, that I wanted to sleep for a month and only wake up to

watch Andy Griffith reruns. It had been an amazing trip. Our team prayed together and hung together through great challenges, and we saw God work. I'll never forget rolling down a dark, endless cobblestone highway at 3:00 a.m. in Transylvania with our team. We were trying to get to the Black Forest Camp after fourteen hours on the plane, twenty hours on the road, and three van breakdowns, with Sister Wanda (a team member from our church) leading us in black gospel choruses to keep us awake. I know I was jet-lagged and delirious at that point . . . but it felt like angels were flying along beside us, forming a grand worship choir and beating back the darkness.

23

Tearful Good-byes

*Love anything and your heart will be wrung
and possibly broken . . . To love is to be vulnerable.*
C.S. Lewis

Our son, Scott, has shared our desire to serve the Lord in Romania. He first came for a short visit in 1996. After his second visit in 1999, he dreamed of bringing folks from the inner city to Romania to minister to the orphans. He fulfilled his dream in the summer of 2000.

Scott wrote this story about his experiences after an exhausting week at camp.

A Time for Lament
by Scott Dewey

The last day of the Loving Arms first camp in the summer of 2000 is one which I will never forget. We organized an evening meeting that would turn out to be so emotional that no one would believe it unless they were there.

The children were extremely fearful about going back to their orphanage after the week at camp. As one Romanian woman described it, "They have had a taste of heaven and now they are going back to hell." They had been crying and clinging to us since the night before. So our team held a prayer meeting in which we laid hands on the children and prayed for God to go with them. The children poured out their emotions with loud sobs and wailing. Some of the Romanian adults seemed uncomfortable with the scene and left, but others later told us how important it was for the children to release their emotions, perhaps for the first time in their lives to such a degree.

Friday evening we loaded the children into the vans and drove them back to their orphanage. They showed us their rooms and we held many in our arms as they cried. Finally, we said good-byes to the children and the staff in the courtyard of their orphanage. The children poured out the pain from their hearts with loud sobs and cries. Our four team leaders left each child with a small gift. Addresses and hugs were exchanged, and with deep emotions we climbed into our vans and waved good-bye.

On saying good-bye, one young boy cried so hard when we were leaving. As I held him in my arms, I realized our tears were mingling and soaking my T-shirt. How can we explain such a response from these children except that God is here and He is at work? This is why I keep coming back.

My granddaughter, Mary, age 18, has traveled to Romania with her dad, Scott, every summer since 2000. Mary speaks Romanian and has developed close relationships with many of the orphans.

Olimpia
by Mary Dewey

Imagine what it is like to be mute. To be silent every day, to never say a word. Sounds escape: grunts, moans, the occasional squeal of laughter. But no words.

I first met her in a Romanian orphanage. She was standing in a hallway corner, rocking. It was no gentle swaying movement; her whole body lurched back and forth, back and forth, her hands held awkwardly in front of her to keep balance. I didn't know she was a girl then, because just like all the other kids, her hair was cut short to keep lice away. I walked toward her and she recoiled, retreating farther into the darkness of the gray walls. "Cum te cheama?" I asked her. "What's your name?" She said nothing.

The first day of summer camp was an explosion of sound. The orphans jumped from the van shouting our names, the names of the "Colorado team." They drowned us in hugs and laughter. They unpacked small bags of belongings that they had managed to keep from the wandering hands of one another. They wanted to tell us everything that had happened to them in the year we were apart, even if some of their stories were not easy to tell. Hands tugged at our shirts, pulling us, begging us for a moment of our time to listen to everything that they had kept inside for so long. But there were two hands that clutched at nothing but air, one voice that did not stir amid the noise. I didn't notice her until the excitement settled, and then I saw her rocking alone. She was good at finding corners. One of the kids told me, "That's Olimpia. She doesn't talk."

> *I didn't notice her until the excitement settled,*
> *and then I saw her rocking alone.*
> *She was good at finding corners.*

I've never been very good with people like her. I have learned some Romanian over the years, and I'm proud of the fact that I can communicate with the kids, but with her my words meant nothing. My dad never seemed to mind, though. He sat with her on that first day, ignoring the chaos around them. She shrank from hugs, so he hugged her gently. She recoiled from touch, so he stroked her short, dark hair. She didn't talk or seem to listen, so he talked to her anyway. She didn't look anyone in the eyes, so he looked at her and told her she was beautiful. It confused the other kids, who reminded him again that she couldn't understand him. He kept on talking. He sang her a song, a tune he made up, with words that repeated over and over. "Olimpia, Olimpia, my little girl."

The week went on, and we saw her smile, then laugh. She clapped perfect time to the music that blasted from a tiny radio. She crammed as much food as she could into her shrunken body. She rocked back and forth, back and forth. And then the day came when the kids piled back into the van amid sobs and good-byes and drove back to the orphanage for another year.

> *She crammed as much food as she could*
> *into her shrunken body.*
> *She rocked back and forth, back and forth.*

The next summer Olimpia was still silent. She still rocked, and she stiffened when I gave her a hug. Another week of camp, another week of music and laughter, and finally we saw that elusive smile that played across her lips when my dad sang her song, "Olimpia, Olimpia, my little girl." He stroked her hand, the one with the deep scar that never really healed because it was the place where she bit herself whenever she was upset.

At first our team thought that maybe a week away from the orphanage, away from the staff that beat her and the kids that taunted her or ignored her, a week full of noise and games and love might let her come alive. But it was such a short amount of time, and after three years we stopped hoping. After a week she always had to go back to the place where she would hide in dark stairwells, in quiet corners where she was no one's little girl.

After three years we stoped hoping.

My dad never stopped talking to her, even during the fourth summer. I'm sure that she understood almost nothing he said to her in English and broken Romanian. He didn't expect her to. That wasn't the point, he said. He just wanted to make her feel special. He sang her song, he talked about work, about the weather, about her eyes. Then he asked her a question, the same question that I asked when I met her four years earlier. "Cum te cheama?" And for the first time in the thirteen years of her life, she spoke. She said, "Olimpia."

I am human. I hear you. I understand you.
I know what love feels like. I can do anything if I feel safe.
I am no longer alone. I am a person. I have a name.

A short while later she said my dad's name, "Scott," the name of her best friend. She didn't say much else that summer, but it didn't matter. We knew she had taken a giant step.

The next year when she got to camp she ran up to me and gave me a hug. I couldn't believe she could do that. I pushed her on the tire swing as she sang camp songs as loud as she could. Her voice exploded into the air, filling up the years of silence. Then she began to hum the tune of her song. *Olimpia, Olimpia, my little girl.* I had so much that she didn't: a loving family, a safe home, friends, a childhood, a future. But there was one thing I had that she had also, if only for a week every year: my father's love. And so despite the chasm between us, she would always be my sister. Sora mea, Olimpia.

My daughter-in-law, Melanie, is a first and second grade teacher in Denver's inner city. Having a strong desire to serve the poor and needy of this world, she served as a missionary in Bangkok for three years with her husband, Scott. She first traveled to Romania in 1998 and joined the Loving Arms team in 2005. Melanie has a tender heart and often seeks out the children with limited mental capacities.

Thorns and Roses
by Melanie Dewey

The van jitters down the winding road packed with both sullen and noisy kids. Kids squished in the back. Kids on laps. Kids pushing my left hip into the metal side of the van. The sullen ones are staring silently at the forest bouncing by. The noisy ones are wailing and reaching out for a spare arm to wrap around their shoulders. Two responses to the same distressing fact: camp is over and it's time to head back to the orphanage.

A few attempts are made to cling to the week we have shared: Remember when the girls beat the boys at tug of war? Remember how nice it was to have pop every day for lunch? Remember all the popcorn Nadia made for us? Remember when Benny shaved his head for that skit? Each memory spoken in hushed tones, like a holy offering.

But then the concrete building looms. We pull into the yard, and the kids collect their plastic bags filled with napkin-wrapped jam sandwiches they had furtively pasted together against coming hunger.

*A few attempts are made to cling
to the week we have shared.
Each memory spoken in hushed tones,
like a holy offering.*

Along the fence stand the kids who weren't at our camp. Dirty feet peek out of cracks in shoes. Hair curls in every direction. Pieces of rope hold up pants that are several sizes too big. I always forget how ragged kids look when they don't have toothbrushes or clothes that match, or someone to hug them and tuck them in at night.

"Come up to my room!" "Come up to my room!" Hands from everywhere grab mine. We head up to the fifth floor. The toilet has been smashed in a past skirmish and is now sitting out on the balcony. Thin, holey blankets stretch across bunks. A music video thumps from the common room's only item of furniture: a tiny TV. "Come dance! Do you know this singer?" More tugs, and it's on to another room. Nothing to tell one room from another, except different kids sitting on the beds.

I find Scott cradling a sobbing Olimpia in her room. Olimpia whose first words—at the age of fourteen—included "Scott." Olimpia, who spends much of her day at camp swinging back and forth on the swing with a wide grin on her face. Olimpia who loved to dance. Wow! Who knew what kind of rhythm she had. Olimpia who talked more than ever this year, even getting ornery with her loudly-expressed opinions. Now she's pouring her grief into Scott's arms.

"Shut up!" the orphanage worker in charge of her floor screams. "I don't want to hear your crying. Shut up!" A loud tirade in Romanian follows. There is no need to understand the individual words to get the meaning. It's back to another year of silence for Olimpia, and now Scott is the one who is sobbing.

> ### *It's back to another year of silence for Olimpia,*
> ### *and now Scott is the one who is sobbing.*

And so we begin our descent into hell. Unlike Jesus, we stand powerless to smash the powers of darkness. We are Lazarus still in the tomb. We are the Hebrew mothers wondering what kind of news whips Herod's soldiers into a frenzy of murder. We are Mary at the foot of the cross watching all our feeble ideas of hope, future, and justice drain away in a red flood.

A boy who betrayed our twelve-year-old son, Christopher's, friendship at camp taunts him in the hallway. Another camper with whom I spent a lot of time comes up to me. I reach up to give him a hug, and he curses loudly at me. The F-word, in English. "Stop," I tell him. But he merely repeats himself. I notice he's wearing a pair of Scott's shorts that he had borrowed earlier in the week. He's off to find another team member to abuse. A hardened defense response to the pain of being back? A mental health issue? Something darker? Definitely one more window into the chaos these kids live with hour by hour in the orphanage.

I want nothing but out. But first I frantically search for the room of my best buddy, Farcas. I can't leave without saying good-bye. I finally find him sitting silently on his bed, staring at the floor between his feet. "I have your picture at home," I tell him. "I promise I will write to you and pray for you every day." I want to ask him to write me, but he can't write. Will someone be kind enough to help him? Who will hold him when he wants to cry? Who will sing with him so he can worship God like he loves to? How will he get to sleep when our team members, Scott or Jim or James, aren't there to pray with him? What will happen to him next summer after he's finished his last year of school?

> ### *Who will hold him when he wants to cry?*
> ### *Who will sing with him*
> ### *so he can worship God like he loves to?*

Thorns and Roses. That's what we call our Loving Arms Team debriefing sessions. Each night at camp—after thirteen hours of intense laughter, lessons, hikes, games, skits, crying, worship, talks—we gather as a ministry team and talk about the things that were hard and the things that were good about the day.

Every day has its challenges. But the thorns we experience when we return the kids to the orphanage—when we allow our hearts to be broken for these dear children—are the hardest. They gash so deeply. Once again, we bleed. More thorns as we pull away in our van, clumps of children chasing after us, wailing. Are these the very thorns entwined around our Savior's brow?

And the roses? The roses turn out to be sunflowers.

The next evening we visit Poiana transit house. Six children from the orphanage were rescued a year ago and now live in a home with a pastor and his family at the end of a dirt road outside the village of Poiana.

The boys cannot wait to show me around the farm. It takes a good deal of time and laughter to realize that the right English word for "big chicks" Radu is so fervently trying to tell me about is "emus." And then there are the rabbits, pigs, dogs, chickens, and rows and rows of cabbages, carrots, tomatoes, cucumbers, and potatoes in the garden. The boys teach our son, Ben, how to use the scythe on the weeds. Miklos explains, by drawing his finger across his throat, what will happen to the pigs at Christmas time. We collapse laughing when we realize the irony of what the pigs have to look forward to at our most anticipated time of year.

> *The thorns we experience when we return the kids*
> *to the orphanage—when we allow our hearts to be broken*
> *for these dear children—are the hardest.*

Across the road from the front porch is a giant field of sunflowers. The sun is dropping into a haze of gold, and we sit in the glow and listen to the hearts of Nelu and Luci, the transit houseparents. It's not been easy. The boys are more accustomed to unpredictable abuse than steady, loving discipline. They're used to taking care of themselves, not following the boundaries of caring parents. "But there is so much they're going to be able to do in life," Nelu says. "Some will start working next year. We'll work hard to help them learn the discipline of showing up to work on time each day. The other boys will be working hard in school. I think some of them could even go on to the university, if we help them work hard in their studies."

And suddenly the rose: This daring man is envisioning a future for these boys! They are not merely a problem, or a challenge, or even a project. They are children of the King, with a future in His kingdom.

This daring man is envisioning a future for these boys!

We pray and dare to hope for a future for forsaken, forgotten children. Yes, we are waiting for the final victory. We beg God every day to fight for these kids—a battle against the forces of darkness—and for the courage to hope for their future. The battle is not over. We feel the thorns. But we battle on, knowing that indeed He has already answered our prayers—the day He became like one of these children and cried out with the pain only an orphan can fully understand, "Father, why have You forsaken me?"

We look forward expectantly for the healing our Savior offers, the healing He offers with His broken, outstretched hands.

Camp's Here

Their joyful cries
Fill every corner
A smile upon each face
Camp's here!

The Bible lessons
That teach God's Word
And heads all bowed in prayer
Camp's begun!

The splashing water
And the small shallow pool
The kids have so much fun
Pool time!

The gentle swinging
And talks with kids
No structure and no form
Free time!

Hilarious skits
They roar with laughter
Boys with make-up on
Afternoon program!

Their voices ringing
With praise to God
In Romanian and English
Evening program!

Darkness falling
It's time for class
With our Professor . . . Gyula
Late night!

Tears of sorrow
Long embraces
I don't want to leave them
camp's ended.

Stifled whimpers
Lengthly letter
It's impossible to wait a year
we're home.

Leann Pulvermiller

24

If A child could Fly

I said, "Oh, that I had wings like a dove!
I would fly away and be at rest."
Psalm 55:6 NASB

Years have passed since Barbro's dream of Casa Alba became a reality, and there are many success stories. Sixty-three children are now living with their adoptive families in Romania and in other countries. Children like Silvia, Gustav, Maria, and Josif have new families.

A few of the severely handicapped children will grow up in a new home, Casa Silvia. Silvia spent several years in Casa Alba. Many times when Lars visited Casa Alba, Silvia would ask, "When will I go to my family?" Sadly, no one would take a child with her autistic-like behavior and learning limitations.

So Lars began to dream again . . . and to pray for a home for Silvia and other handicapped children. Before long, sponsors provided needed funds, and Lars renovated a large two-story house that became Casa Silvia. A dedicated staff looks after the many needs of Silvia and other special needs children. Because these children also needed a school, FCE started the first school for the handicapped and mentally challenged children in Marghita. Special needs children from Marghita and the surrounding villages attend.

Some children have been placed in loving foster homes. One of these was Josif, a silent little boy with searching eyes who I met in the hospital. At two years of age, he could not walk. His legs extended at strange angles . . . possibly because he lay in a crib all day. One day when I went to Casa Alba, Josif was not there. His parents came and took him home. Some months later, they brought him to the hospital in very poor condition. His thin body showed the bruises of the abuse he suffered.

Josif was placed with a foster family in a village 25 km from Marghita. When Josif was school age, his foster mom, Luminita, enrolled him in the village school. He did not adjust well to the structure of a regular classroom, and his behavior was out of control. Josif could not continue in school. So Luminita decided to see if the FCE special school could help him. Twice a week, they walked down a long and often muddy road to catch a bus to Marghita to take Josif to school. On the other days, she helped him with school assignments at home. She says, "As long as he is at home with our family, he is no problem." In 2006, Josif's family moved closer to Marghita, and now he is able to attend the special school every day.

While Iorela Karlsson was director of Casa Alba, a frail little baby was abandoned in Marghita Hospital. His dark eyes and long eyelashes were his most distinguishing features. He was severely malnourished and weak. Dr. Yacoob, the hospital's head pediatrician, allowed Gustav to be moved to Casa Alba where he would receive good care. Iorela could not resist this little boy, especially since he had the same name as a Swedish king. It did not take long for Gustav and Iorela to become "in love" with each other. When Iorela would enter Casa Alba, Gustav would yell, "Iorela, Iorela," and jump into her arms.

In the loving atmosphere of Casa Alba and with good nutrition, Gustav began to thrive.

Each time she left for the day, Iorela would have a talk with Gustav. "I have to go now, but I will be back in the morning," she would tell him. Amazingly enough, Gustav was resigned to the fact that he would not see her until the next day. In the loving atmosphere of Casa Alba and with good nutrition, Gustav began to thrive. In time, he was healthy and energetic just like any two-year-old.

I was home in Denver when I received an e-mail from Iorela. The unthinkable had happened. Gustav's parents came back and took him home with them. Iorela wrote, "I keep his picture on my desk. Each time I look at Gustav's picture I cry."

It seemed hopeless that Iorela would ever see Gustav again. Her dream of adopting him was dashed. Yet another miracle! Gustav's parents decided not to keep him and brought him back to Casa Alba. Excitement was in the air when Gustav came back. Now Iorela could proceed with her dream of adopting Gustav and one day taking him back to Sweden as her son.

Adoption by foreigners is never easy in Romania especially for single women. The judge vacillated back and forth. At one moment Iorela thought that all the documents were completed and she could adopt Gustav. In the next hearing, the judge changed his mind. These torturous days continued on and on. Gustav constantly asked Iorela if he could go home with her. He really wasn't her son, yet. She hesitated to take him for fear that the adoption would not go through. Finally, Iorela could wait no longer, and Gustav went to live with her in her apartment.

Gustav is now a Swedish-speaking teenager with a loving "forever" mother.

During this anxious time, Iorela's emotions were raw. Meanwhile Iorela and a fine Christian woman, Lidia Micula, shared the responsibility of directing the work at Casa Alba. When it was time for Iorela to leave, Lidia would assume the responsibility of director. I prayed daily for Gustav to soon be Iorela's little boy.

Finally, one day it happened. This was a joyous moment for all of us, but also bittersweet as we realized that this would mean Iorela would return to Sweden. Gustav is now a Swedish-speaking teenager with a loving "forever" mother.

Maria lived without a family until she was six.

She longed to leave like the other children and go to a family of her own. Finally, a family was found, and when she was told, Maria's excitement bubbled over. Soon she joined the family with their two younger daughters, and she was welcomed warmly.

In October 2004, Fred and I taught a seminar for foster parents, and Maria's foster mother came to the classes. After the last class, she invited us to her home to meet Maria. Wow! What a change in this little girl since we saw her years before in Casa Alba. She had become a smiling and somewhat shy young lady of twelve. Lavinia, our translator, introduced us and told Maria that we used to care for her in Marghita Hospital and in Casa Alba. Maria showed me some of her schoolwork. Her mother said that school is difficult for Maria, but she does very well in some subjects.

During her first year with her family, Maria's adjustment was stressful. She was very fearful. Living in a family was a totally new experience, and she had no idea how to relate to a mother, father, and sisters. What does a mother do? Who are sisters? How do you share a mother . . . or share anything else? With time, Maria bonded with her new family, and they all came to love one another.

As we talked to her mother, Maria brought out a stack of photographs of her childhood years. We went through them one-by-one, and we finally came to one picture of me holding her in the hospital. She was thrilled! She could not stop talking. As we prepared to leave, she asked when we would come again.

Years ago, when I prayed for a family for Maria, God already had one in His plan.

There was a very special boy in Casa Alba named Valentin.

He was adopted by a wonderful Christian family from Connecticut—Andrew, Sandra, and Katelynn Lee. Recently I e-mailed Sandra and asked for an update on the boy we knew as Valentin.

His new name is Justin. Sandra sent me photos and wrote the following letter.

Dear Karleen:

It is so great to hear from you—Justin is doing so well—he is the sweetest boy and is a real American boy. I will try and e-mail you some photos if you would like, and I would love a copy of the book for him. He will be thirteen years old in March, and he is in the sixth grade attending Christian Heritage School. He loves to sing and cook—he plays the piano and percussion in the school band. He also plays soccer, basketball and baseball. He is a true gift from God, and we are so grateful to Casa Alba for housing him until God sent us to adopt him. He has been such a blessing to our entire family and we talk about someday going back to visit Romania as a family.

Sandra wrote that Justin was asked to give a speech for National Pledge of Allegiance Day at his school. His family was glowing with pride as he stood before a large audience and gave his speech.

Buna Dimineata. In Romanian, that means, "Good Morning."

My name is Justin Valentin Lee and I was born on March 12, 1994, in Marghita, Romania. I will never forget the day that my Papa came to visit me during Christmas 1999. That was the "BEST" Christmas present any boy could have ever asked for. Little did I know that he would be bringing my entire new family in approximately five months back to Romania to pick me up and take me to America. I was waiting a very long time for them to come back. You can imagine that a boy at age six does not have much patience.

On April 15, 2000, God delivered two wonderful parents and a beautiful sister who adopted me and brought me back to America. That's when I officially became an American citizen or as my family calls me their "American boy."

When I arrived in America, I could not speak one word of English; however, in seven months I was fluent in the language.

I feel so special that God gave me a new life in America and to be able to experience all of the opportunities that our country has to offer.

In Matthew 19:14 Jesus said, "Let the little children come to me, and do not hinder them for the Kingdom of God belongs to them."

Diane Pulvermiller came to Romania in 2001

with the Colorado Loving Arms team to run a camp in the Black Forest. Diane discovered a special place her heart for a fourteen-year-old orphan named Gyula who was on the verge of being sent to a larger orphanage with older, abusive teens. He was very afraid.

The Loving Arms team and the FCE volunteers prayed along with many others. It seemed like a terrible injustice to have a gentle, fun-loving boy like Gyula live in a harsh orphanage environment. Then, in the summer of 2003, the exciting news she longed to hear came in the form of an e-mail.

> Dear Diane . . .
>
> I want to tell that I am here now in Marghita with my [foster] mom by God's help. I want to thank you so much . . . I don't know where to start to thank God for this. [Signed]Gyula.

What follows is Diane's account of these remarkable events.

For sixteen years Gyula lived in government run Romanian orphanages. This last summer, we were able to place Gyula in a foster home with a woman he loves and now calls "Mom." Here is Gyula's story.

I've known Gyula for three years now. He has been at camp with us for several summers. This past summer I really had a chance to get to know him better and we really bonded. Saying good-bye really tore my heart out.

After arriving back home, I could not stop thinking about him and the new school he would be sent to in the fall. It was in the city and is a place rampant with physical and sexual abuse. I really felt the Lord's call to do something, but I didn't know what the something looked like.

I checked into the possibility of adopting him but discovered five days after his sixteenth birthday that the US government no longer recognizes children as orphans once they turn sixteen. With that door shut I contacted Alisha Inch in Romania. Alisha is a Canadian who has been working with the kids in a local orphanage for four years now. I asked her if there could be any way we could get Gyula fostered if the funds were available.

After much prayer and discussion with the FCE leadership, Alisha got back to me and let me know that she would love to take Gyula in. When I heard that, my heart jumped. I knew that's what God wanted! Alisha and Gyula have a very special relationship since she first started working with the kids.

So Alisha began the process to gain custody. Things seem to be moving along. The final step was to get the okay from Child Protective Services in Romania. When Alisha arrived at the office, she discovered that Gyula's paperwork had already been started to move him to where his mother was living. Abandoned at birth, his parents had never seen him. This county in southern Romania was seven hours away from Marghita.

Gyula (on left) with Alisha is no longer an orphan—he has a home!

Needless to say, Alisha and Gyula were devastated. They had no idea when Gyula's move would occur. Until his papers were completed, it looked like he would have to attend the huge and dangerous school in the city.

To my surprise, the next week I heard from Alisha that the social workers were going to move Gyula in a few days. His parents had officially signed off on him, so he would just be moved to a new institution in a town far away. Alisha planned to travel with him to help him get settled. Also going were the social worker from FCE, Diana, and a state social worker.

When they arrived, Diana said she would go in and see if there was any way for Gyula to stay with Alisha. Five minutes later she came back out and said there was no way it could happen. They unloaded Gyula's things and started walking into the building. Just as they entered, the state social worker said to Gyula, "If you want to, you can go." They sat down in complete shock, filled out some papers, and drove seven hours back to Marghita.

Gyula is no longer an orphan—he has a home!

Back in Colorado, I just went crazy! It is all from God. I prayed whatever the outcome, His glory would shine, and that is exactly what happened. This is an impossible outcome. Only God made Gyula's life turn out this way. So that's the story. One I never get tired of telling.

Gyula is eighteen and lives now with his foster mom and her parents in British Columbia. He plans to return to Romania sometime in the future.

God worked in the life of Tomi,

a tall, handsome young man, in some amazing ways. Tomi was befriended by a Christian family who lived near his orphanage. They invited him to stay in their home on weekends, and he had the opportunity to observe healthy family relationships. This family modeled practical Christian living for Tomi. Each time he returned to the orphanage, Tomi felt disheartened. More and more, he longed for a good family.

In 2005, Tomi wrote to me. "Fortunately a small organization in England heard of the situation and took me out of the orphanage and allowed me to live by myself in an apartment until I finished high school. I am probably the first person from my orphanage to finish a normal high school course and take end-of-school exams, finishing with high marks. When I have had time, I also like to help people less fortunate than I am. I have spent time with other orphans, giving them the opportunity to get away from the institution, even for a day, and have tried to reach out to some of the elderly people in my community."

After graduation, Tomi earned money as a taxi driver for several years. He served as a translator and a worship leader at the Loving Arms summer camps. Tomi is gifted in playing the guitar. My pastor and his wife, Jim and Barb Demolar, have served on the camp teams for several summers. Barb and Tomi have developed a mother-son relationship, and Barb has been a profound influence in Tomi's life. Now he lives in Landsend, England, where he is working in construction. He lives there with the family that has supported him all these years.

I asked Tomi if he worries about his future. "Sometimes. But I know I have people who are praying for me. This is special . . . I have God."

Zoli's story has many twists and turns. He is a student in social work at the University of Oradea. Zoli enjoys many friends and is a really happy guy. I still look at him in amazement. He is a handsome young man—clean shaven, with a nicely trimmed haircut and a few dark curls on the top, and a college prep look to his clothes. What is ahead in his future?

Zoli hopes to help parentless boys and girls such as him have a better life. In a casual way, he shares the story of the hardships and disappointments he faced and how God transformed his life.

His success story motivates me to continue to be involved in the orphans' lives. Where would this formerly "ragamuffin orphan" be without Barbro, Sofia, Cici, and others who came to love him and share the good news of Jesus Christ. I pray there will be more "Zoli's" in the future. Zoli is in love and hopes to marry. It is wonderful to know that in the future Zoli will have his own family.

Imi and I have a relationship which has lasted thirteen years.
I see him almost every day going to or from work.

While living in Cadea, Imi was trained by Phyllis Parker to become a hairstylist. He worked under Phyllis in a salon that she set up with the help of FCE.

After three years, Phyllis returned home to Colorado. Imi and his partner, Koliman, started up their own salon. They are now Marghita businessmen.

Imi fell in love and married a wonderful young woman, Csilla. As a young girl, Csilla, was also in an orphanage. Csilla and Imi have their own very attractive house in the village of Chiribis. It is a joy to visit this couple that might not have been except for the grace of God.

We thank God that some of the orphans came out of the orphanage system and found freedom to "fly away." Many have gone to other parts of the world and joined eager families waiting for them. Wounds are healing and broken wings are mending. These former orphans have joy in their sparkling eyes and love in their hearts. I will never forget their stories as they are proof that love can shine brightly through the darkness.

I will never forget their stories as they are proof
that love can shine brightly through the darkness.

If A Child Could Fly
An Ode to Romania's Orphans

If a child could fly,
Soaring upward he would go
Never to return.

His sorrowing heart weeps,
Love lacking erodes the soul.
Why would he remain?

Soaring heaven bound,
The flame of hope burns within.
Come, I'll fly with you.

25

Glimpes from
My Heart

I pray that the eyes of your heart may be enlightened . .
Ephesians 1:18 NASB

Superman
Summer 1993

It's a bird. It's a plane. It's . . . ?

Try as I might I did not see Superman. As the hot noon sun beat down on my head, all I saw was a dismal-looking patch of ground with trampled weeds and broken glass surrounded by an old wooden fence. Forty dirty, skinny little boys wandered about, scratching the dirt or simply standing silently.

"Over there," pointed the boy who I had taken into my arms. "Over there is Superman. And over there" he motioned grandly toward an empty corner of the lot, "is God."

At that moment I longed for the imagination of this little seven-year-old boy who I would soon nickname "Superman." For him, the orphanage play yard is a place where Superman, in his long blue cape, leaps from the tallest buildings and swoops down into the yard. God, too, is in *His* corner. I wonder, *What is God doing here?*

This was the Loving Arms team's first visit to this orphanage. This region of southern Romania had received almost no assistance from the West. During our visit we hoped simply to establish rapport with the staff, make friends, and offer future assistance.

Our team had visited many orphanages over the past three years. We had seen heartbreaking sights. We were prepared to see needy children, or so we thought.

This orphanage was a shock!

Our Romanian translator, a local man, was as stunned as we were. "God forbid," he kept repeating. This sun-baked, shadeless courtyard would be unfit for animals, let alone children. The boys were covered with cuts and bruises—evidence that whatever play they could manage often turned violent. They wore dirty, ragged clothes and mismatched shoes, or none at all. A lone staff person, whose role seemed to me merely that of a bouncer, jerked the boys by their arms when gruff commands drew no response.

This orphanage was a shock!

We stayed for several hours, gathering information from the staff but mostly playing with the children. The boys clung to us the entire time, pleading for attention. They bruised our arms in their desperate attempts to make physical contact. Off against the wooden fence, a few orphans who were clearly emotionally disturbed rocked slowly back and forth.

When it was time to go, we finally pulled ourselves away. The children hung on the fence trying to get one last pat or smile. My eyes searched for Superman. Finally, I saw him, not with the cluster of boys at the fence, but over against the building. He had laid his thin arm up on the wall and put his face against the concrete. He was crying in uncontrollable sobs.

It was all I could do to fight back my twisting emotions
and the sudden urge just to pick up this child
and snatch him away from this wretched place.

It was all I could do to fight back my twisting emotions and the sudden urge just to pick up this child and snatch him away from this wretched place. Silently we all piled into our van and drove away. Through my own tears I saw Superman shuffle slowly back toward the playground.

Back home, I wondered, *Why did Superman cry when we left? We were there such a short time—much shorter than at the other orphanages we visited. Could he sense that we cared for him?*

Somehow, I hoped that Superman understood that God in the corner of the playground truly loves him.

"We were trained to teach normal children.
These children have many problems.
We need information on how to help these children.
No one has ever come to help us."
Orphanage caregiver, southern Romania

the Place of the mourning Doves ~ 182

Gypsy Eyes
Summer 1997

Two little, blond Gypsy girls came running out from a rickety wooden gate. They smiled a welcome to us. Stunning! Two pairs of the most beautiful eyes sparkled like stars. The girls held out their hands beckoning us into their yard. Another sister shyly hung back near the doorway. A toddler clung to her sister's skirt. Signs of poverty were everywhere . . . yet the yard and small stucco house were surprisingly neat. A long line of hand-scrubbed laundry was drying in the morning sun.

The girls spoke in Romanian to my Swedish friend, Linda, who translated for us. Their mother, Maria, was not home.

Linda told us that this was a very unusual Gypsy family. Maria grew up in the orphanage system after being abandoned by her parents. She spent years in a nearby orphanage in this very village.

From my experiences in orphanages, I knew the chances were slim that an orphan would learn how to be a nurturing mother in that environment.

After her orphanage years, Maria was married and had seven children. Undoubtedly, she felt some pressure to leave her children in an orphanage just as her mother did, but her impoverished background only seemed to strengthen her resolve to provide a loving home for her children. She was determined to take good care of her family.

Linda visited Maria in this Gypsy village over a period of several years. The two women cultivated a close friendship.

Maria struggled to keep her family fed and clothed. Winters are hard in Romania, and it is difficult to keep warm.

Though Gypsies are not often open to friendships with outsiders, we were welcomed in this village. What a delightful time we had in this home, and we were captivated by the children. We left some food and clothing. I felt sorry that I did not meet their wonderful mother, but in the children's eyes I saw the results of her loving care.

***Though Gypsies are not often open
to friendships with outsiders,
we were welcomed in this village.***

His Kingdom Come
Winter 1999

It was January in Romania, and the huge concrete building was freezing cold. I could see my breath inside. The hall was dark except for one bare lightbulb. Green, peeling paint covered the filthy walls. Rusty metal stair railings led to the upper floors. A musty smell of mold and urine reached my nose. The ugliness of my surroundings made me shudder. Beauty was utterly absent from this place.

> *The ugliness of my surroundings made me shudder.*
> *Beauty was utterly absent from this place.*

Shadowy figures lurked in the darkness. Several grimy-looking orphans grabbed my arms. I felt overwhelmed as they jabbered, "Come see my room. Come see my room."

Almost two hundred teen orphans lived in this miserable place in the small village of Cadea. Many of the abandoned children's parents lived in nearby villages. Most of these orphans were boys, but there were a few masculine-looking girls. All the girls had short haircuts and deep voices. It was impossible for me to tell whether I was talking to a girl or boy. At that moment, I felt a burden of hopelessness for the orphans who lived here. I asked myself, *Is it possible that any of these kids could ever have a decent life?*

> *Is it possible that any of these kids*
> *could ever have a decent life?*

On both sides of the hall were rows of bedrooms—eight kids to a room. One of the more gregarious teens pulled me into his room. He was so proud of it, but all I could see was the poverty these kids lived in. They slept on smelly, crumbling foam mattresses. Only the lucky ones had threadbare blankets. Younger and weaker children had none. Each child had a small cabinet for his meager belongings, locked to keep them from being stolen by others.

I felt a blast of cold air rushing through a broken window, a casualty of a fit of rage by one of the boys. No one had bothered to fix it. In fact, no one bothered themselves about the orphans except the Christian volunteers. If there was a night attendant, he was not around. The older, tough bullies ruled. We heard rumors that the staff paid the bullies to control the group.

I had not wanted to go to Cadea that night. I felt uncomfortable—unsafe, to be honest. The dim light and dark shadows made me feel I had entered a draconian dungeon.

Yet this was a very special night. A small group of boys had asked Dan Micula, the pastor of three village churches, to come to speak to them about prayer. The boys planned to have a Bible study and time of worship in one of the bedrooms. We were invited to join them along with some other volunteers. The room was crowded. One small lightbulb hanging from the ceiling gave the boys' faces a golden glow.

I had not wanted to go to Cadea that night.
I felt uncomfortable—unsafe, to be honest.

When I entered the room, one of the boys immediately jumped up and gave me his seat on a bed. Kids snuggled up to each of the adults as they found a place to sit on the floor or a bed. Boys leaned against each of my shoulders. What a strange-looking bunch! We had on our warm down jackets and insulated boots. In their futile attempt to keep warm, the kids wore several layers of ragged clothes, well-worn shoes, and no socks.

Pastor Dan spoke on the power of God to change each life in the room. He explained the Lord's Prayer. The room was hushed, and we bowed our heads for prayer. Tears came to my eyes as a number of the boys prayed. I could understand enough of the Romanian words to know they were praying for their friends who had come from America. Several of the boys began to play guitars and we sang worship songs, some in Romanian and some in English.

I looked around the room as we huddled together praising the Lord God Almighty. In these brief moments of taking it all in, God reminded me that this was truly *His Kingdom* . . . the *Kingdom of God*. Before my eyes, the room took on a warm, rich glow. God was in our midst. This was an unforgettable *holy* and *sacred* moment. Because of my anxiety, I almost missed it.

God brought me to this unlikely place
and gave me a glimpse of heaven.

As I walked out of the building and into the darkness, I could hear songs of praise flowing through the orphanage. For a few minutes, I stood in the snow in awe of what God had done on this night. My heart was filled with hope for the children. God brought me to this unlikely place and gave me a glimpse of heaven.

One orphan boy, now grownup, said,

"While my mother might slap me, the staff beat me with a stick."
He is the same boy who said, "I am glad I was in the orphanage
because that is where I heard about Jesus
from the volunteers who came to visit."

Happy Eyes
Spring 2002

Cornelius was not the prettiest baby at Marghita Hospital. In fact, the nurses paid him little attention.

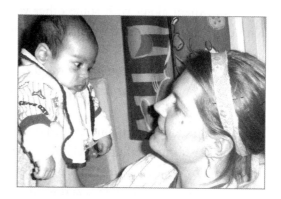

Cornelius was not the prettiest baby at Marghita Hospital. In fact, the nurses paid him little attention. He was very small with a misshapen head that made him look lopsided. "I called him my little 'tweety bird,'" said Courtney Brown, a Mercy Ministries volunteer serving in Romania. Cornelius stole Courtney's heart. He had spent most of his short life in a crib in the hospital. Now he just sat there rocking himself all day.

Courtney went to play with Cornelius every day. It was hard for her to see him suffer. She cried to God to heal him. Soon he started to be more responsive and even greeted her with a smile. One evening, Courtney noticed that Cornelius had a fever. He laid his little head on Courtney's shoulder and fell sound asleep. She held him for over an hour, feeling grateful she could comfort him. Then, carefully, she put him back to bed whispering, "Okay, God, watch him tonight while he is sick."

*He had spent most of his short life
in a crib in the hospital.
Now he just sat there rocking himself all day.*

Later that year, Cornelius was moved to Casa Alba. There he had plenty of room to play and was no longer confined to his crib. He is now two years old and thriving. Courtney says, "Now he just smiles with happy eyes. He is my favorite kid, and I want to take him home with me."

In the past five years, Courtney has opened her heart to the orphans of Romania. When she first went to Marghita with the 1996 Loving Arms team, she could hardly bear the suffering she saw. Each night, she would pray for the children. Tiny, frail, and underfed abandoned babies were sorely neglected in Marghita Hospital.

When Courtney returned home to Colorado after her first trip to Romania, she couldn't forget the orphans, especially the "little ones." God placed in her heart a desire to go back and be part of the solution for the orphans. Since then Courtney has divided her time between Romania and Colorado. After caring for dozens of babies, she has seen firsthand the damage neglect can do to a child.

> *The high point of Courtney's week is a time of prayer*
> *with the international team of volunteers.*

Yet babies are not Courtney's only interest in Romania. God has touched her heart with love for the teen orphans—especially the girls. Cadea is the last place some orphans go before being sent out to fend for themselves. It is a despicable, unheated, and unsupervised place. The Cadea teens are a pitiful and scruffy bunch. Every week, Courtney visits four girls who were placed together with fifty boys. These girls are tough and "in your face." Courtney says, "I think they really feel overwhelmed and fearful of the boys." Her prayer is that "the girls will come to know how much I love them and that they will be moved to a safer place." She would like to see the girls with "happy eyes," too.

The high point of Courtney's week is a time of prayer with the international team of volunteers. "We share our hearts. It's so special to worship in different languages and to know we are one in our love for God." It's God's love that gives Courtney the desire to go back to care for the orphans . . . again and again.

Yellow Shoes
Fall 2006

As I sat in church, I looked at the shoes of the boy sitting next to me. They were on the wrong feet. Of course, all young children sometimes put their shoes on wrong. However, Dacian is not a young child. He is twelve and an orphan. He has no mother or staff person who cares enough to say, "Dacian, you have your shoes on the wrong feet. Take them off and put them on right." At one point, Dacian bowed his head and with his hands clasped, prayed fervently. What was his prayer? When he looked up, I noticed his wet eyelashes. Something in this time of prayer touched his heart,

About fifty orphans sat scattered throughout the small congregation. What an unusual church.

Several blocks away is the orphanage where about one hundred thirty children live. This was a sad day for many of the children who, tomorrow, will go to a larger orphanage to begin their ninth year of school. Many are fearful about their future, as was one girl who sat in our row at church. Tears dripped down her cheeks throughout the whole service. It reminded me of something out of a Dickens' novel where children were beaten because they asked for more food.

Another pair of shoes caught my eye. Roxana never had on shoes that match. This time, she had a blue flip-flop on one foot and a pink one on the other. Last week, she had on one tennis shoe and one sandal. Does the pile of shoes she sorts through not have matching pairs? Do mean kids steal her shoes? If I ask her, she will be "rusine" or embarrassed, so I don't ask. I try to focus on her beautiful smile. Sometime and somewhere, someone carved a cross on her forehead. The scar is still there. Roxana looks twelve, but she is seventeen. Tomorrow she will go to another orphanage, and I might see her once a month.

Roxana never had on shoes that match.

Romi, a fifteen-year-old orphan, wore bright yellow tennis shoes from spring to mid-summer. Last spring, Fred and I moved into our apartment in Marghita. Now that we are retired, we are living here for an extended period. We invited Romi to come visit us, and he wore leather shoes without socks. The holes in the bottoms of his shoes were so big that they ruined any socks he wore. Fred tried to patch the insides with cardboard, and when this didn't work, we looked in FCE's storage depot. There, sitting in a box, was a pair of brand new yellow tennis shoes. Romi was thrilled! He promised to give them back to the depot as soon as he received new shoes from the Loving Arms camp team.

Romi came to visit again in June. As soon as he walked in the door, I noticed a strong odor that I quickly discovered came from his shoes which were hardly yellow anymore. After going through several buckets of water, we finally got them clean. When they were dry, we discovered that they, too, were falling apart.

"A man on the street asked to buy my shoes, but I said no because I promised to bring them back," Romi said.

I was delighted when the camp team from Colorado gave Romi new shoes and socks.

I pray for the day when all of "God's children" have shoes . . .
not worn-out ones, not mismatched ones, not smelly yellow ones,
but brand new shoes.

New Kids On the Block
Fall 2006

I want to share parts of the wonderful day we had yesterday. FCE has three transit homes, each with houseparents and six teen orphans. Each year, there are a few spaces as older ones move on to our program called "Final Help." This year, we have seven spaces.

All the papers were completed for seven teen orphans to enter the transit homes. The children were so excited to finally be leaving the orphanage. The third week of August the director of the orphanage told the kids they would be moving into the transit homes September 1. All was well and anticipation continued to grow as the days passed. A week later, the director dropped a bombshell. She told the kids they could not move after all. Because of a new rule, only those older than eighteen could move into the transit homes. We were stunned, and the kids were devastated. Six of the children were under eighteen. We met with the kids and cried and prayed with them.

During the intervening time, Florin Costea tried to make appointments with authorities in Oradea. The meetings were scheduled and then cancelled because someone had to be out of town. Each time we went to the orphanage we would tell the kids, "Lars and Florin are fighting for you." Two weeks passed, September 1 came and went, and the kids were giving up hope. They thought their opportunity to leave the orphanage had gone with the wind.

They thought their opportunity to leave the orphanage had gone with the wind.

Yesterday there was an important meeting of the Child Protection Committee in Oradea. Florin was listed first on the meeting agenda. The head of Child Protection for Bihor County was there. He listened very carefully to Florin's presentation, and he agreed that all of the teens should be moved. The committee agreed, too. Best of all, they could be moved right away!

Three of the teens had already been sent to a large orphanage in Oradea to begin their ninth year of school. After the meeting, Florin stopped at their school and brought them to Marghita. Five of us went with Lars to the orphanage to get the other children. Oh how excited the children were!

They had packed their meager belongings into bags and said good-bye to the other kids who, of course, were very sad to be left behind. Some of the teachers came to say good-bye and wish them well. A few were given hugs. The kids shouted "la revedere" as we pulled away. During the thirty-minute drive to Marghita, the kids sang praise songs, thanking God for intervening in their lives.

When we arrived at the foundation office in Marghita, shouts of joy erupted. The houseparents were there to hug the kids. We all celebrated. When Fred walked in, the kids hugged him, and I could see the emotion in his eyes.

After crowding into the conference room, everyone ate bonbons and drank orange pop. The kids told how they had given up hope. Alex shared that when the bus came to take him to the high school, he felt like this was the end. Riding on the bus, he kept praying to God to give him a miracle.

Sitting between Fred and me, one boy was his typical high-spirited self. I whispered in his ear, "You are no longer an orphan." A few moments later, he began to sob. No more living in fear. Now he is part of a family. Lars and Florin gave some words of advice, much of it was in Romanian, and the kids nodded their heads in agreement. It was such a joyous and emotional time.

> *Sitting between Fred and me,*
> *one boy was his typical high-spirited self.*
> *I whispered in his ear, "You are no longer an orphan."*
> *A few moments later, he began to sob. No more living in fear.*
> *Now he is part of a family.*

Romi and Karleen

I suggested we find a large flat rock and etch on it the date—September 18, 2006—as a memorial to what God did on this day. In the Old Testament, the Jewish folks built a pile of stones in remembrance of God's miracle.

There are new kids on the block at Poiana farm, in the village of Chiribis, and in the town of Marghita. May the Lord be praised.

> *For I am confident of this very thing,*
> *that He who began a good work in you*
> *will perfect it until the day of Christ Jesus.*
>
> Philippians 1:6 NASB

26

Journey toward Healing

*The LORD is near to the brokenhearted
And saves those who are crushed in spirit.*

Psalm 34:18 NASB

How do you end a story that has not ended? I cannot truthfully write "and they lived happily ever after." Even when Prince Charming enters the story, the heart's deepest wounds may remain.

Each abandoned child must go on his own journey toward healing. Some will make it and others won't. Some orphans bear deep emotional scars, and their relationships may be destroyed before they have a chance to blossom. Other orphans will impulsively make choices which will further destroy their hearts. Addictions are an easy out for those who choose to bury their pain. Tragically, a few children have been so hardened by the system that they shrug their shoulders and say, "What pain? I don't have any pain."

How many years will it take for a child to learn the "hard way" that life doesn't work according to his way? One of our adopted sons, now in his thirties, said, "I feel like I have wasted twenty-five years of my life." The choices he made led to addictions and jail time. He would love to take back those years . . . to redeem them . . . but that's impossible!

I look at the young men and women in the transit homes who are in their late teens. They will be on their own in a year or two. Will they be able to make the journey toward a life full of loving relationships? I don't know, but with a few of them I see a door opening to a life of hope. What makes the difference? Why does one child make choices that destroy his life and another child choose to live life to the fullest?

Orphans who acknowledge their victimization but who decide not to get "stuck" there seem to move along a path toward healing. Some dream of a future, while others plan for their future. Perhaps they will learn a vocational skill or obtain further education.

An essential element of the healing process is learning to love others. When they can love others unselfishly and give without expecting to receive, they are ready to face life as a mature adult.

Am I looking for some type of utopia? I think not. Do I believe loving relationships are possible for a wounded orphan? I do. Life will be a struggle, and it will take a courageous heart to keep on loving when confronted with the disappointments of life. Knowing that they are loved and that they have value is critically important.

Many of these children have expressed their faith in God. They have made a personal decision to follow Jesus. They feel His Spirit in their very souls. I hear them pray, and I sense the depth of their relationship with Him. Yet not every child who says, "I believe in Jesus," will find his life immediately transformed. Maybe it will take years for this faith to take root, as it has for our son. However, I have witnessed softened and changed hearts that can only be the result of Jesus' love and forgiveness in their lives.

Without God, there is no way anyone can change a heart that is walled in with bricks of betrayal and mistrust. No way. But Jesus said, "I am the way, and the truth and the life" (John 14:6 NASB). We are not talking about cleaning up kids with bad attitudes from nice families in suburban US. We are talking about kids who have been battered, raped, sodomized, and called every degrading name in the book. Some have committed these crimes against weaker children. Left alone, and without love, these children have no destiny but to self-destruct.

Isn't it interesting that God's words say we must love Him first, then ourselves, and then others. God tells us in simple terms the way to a new heart. It's like choosing life over death.

Is there the possibility that such a child can live "happily *ever after*?" Yes, but not yet. *Ever after* comes to all of us when the journey is over. For our beloved orphans, the journey has just begun. The end is just the beginning.

For our beloved orphans, the journey has just begun. The end is just the beginning.

Questions & A Few Answers

Q: Would it be better to bring the orphans to the United States?

A. The focus should be on getting the children into caring families no matter what country they will live in. The children are Romanian. If good Romanian families can be found, they can develop fully in their own country. Some children do require special services not yet available in Romania. It is my opinion these children should be allowed to go wherever they can receive adequate treatment. At this time, international adoptions are not allowed, so we must find good Romanian families for the children.

Q: Instead of spending a lot of money to send a team, why don't you just send money to help the children?

A. We do both. However, the children need relationships with people who will love them. These loving relationships have come from Romanian staff, foreign volunteers, and teams who come to run the camps. Another factor is that God works changes in the hearts of the people who come. They go home with a better understanding of what it is to love a needy child. Many Romanians are very kind to the children, but to give themselves as full-time volunteers is not possible here for economic reasons.

Q: Is the orphans' situation getting better?

A. Yes, when you compare it to what it was like when we first came in 1991. The children get more food and have better clothes. There are fewer orphanages, and more children have been placed in families. More Romanians are willing to be adoptive or foster parents. There is a government allowance for each child. In one state orphanage nearby, a new director is working to improve the facilities and the care of the children.

Q. What is the current situation at Marghita Hospital?

A. Conditions are better for the babies, and fewer babies are being abandoned. There are seven babies in the hospital now, and the number changes week by week. Child Protection is finding foster families for some of these babies. Others go back to their families as soon as Child Protection or the doctors determine that the home life is stable and suitable for the babies' welfare. The babies look well fed. There is a shortage of nurses which means the babies still lack adequate care and nurture from hospital staff.

FCE has hired full-time caregivers, and we have volunteers who go regularly. One volunteer, Courtney Brown, has worked in the hospital for ten years. When a baby is reunited with a family, Courtney often goes to the village to see how the baby is developing. Also, Marghita Hospital has a part-time social worker who visits the home of each abandoned baby.

Q. How many children are at Casa Alba? Are you finding families willing to adopt them?

A. There now twenty children in Casa Alba from ages three to eight. Lidia Micula has been the director of Casa Alba since Iorela left in 2000. Lidia interviews potential Romanian families interested in adoption or foster care. In partnership, FCE and Mercy Ministries have a Family Friends (child sponsorship) program whereby the children are financially supported when they go into foster homes.

Q. What happened to Cadea and the orphans who lived there?

A. Perhaps God said, "No more." The director of Cadea died suddenly and Cadea orphanage was closed. There is still a home for handicapped young people in the village called Cadea Camin. Two FCE volunteers visit the residents two afternoons a week and provide a program for small groups. Otherwise, no activities are planned for these people by the staff.

The orphans from Cadea are all in their twenties now. Some went to the streets, some to our transit houses, and others have integrated into various communities. One is studying at the university in Oradea, and another is in prison. Alcohol has taken its toll on a few who have never settled down with one job or one place to live. A really tough guy in Cadea who was cruel to the other children and had a drinking problem has straightened out his life. Barbro reports that he is married, has children, and is doing well.

Q: What happens to the older teens who leave the orphanage?

A. The teens who are fortunate to be supported by a private foundation or by concerned individuals learn skills and adjust into Romanian society. However, often the residual affects of living for years in an institution remain throughout adult life. Other teens have nowhere to go but to the streets. Very few return to their birth families. A few are able to find low paying jobs in shoe factories or something similar. It is very difficult for Gypsy orphans to find good jobs. Now that Romania is in the European Union, many will seek work abroad.

Q: Does FCE still have transit homes?

A. Yes, FCE has three transit homes, two for boys and one for girls. Seven children live in each home. All these children either attend school or have jobs.

Q: How do you know what stories to believe that the children tell?

A. We have all asked this question. When I see the whole picture over sixteen years, I realize the orphans' stories are true. We have close relationships with some of the children, and we are confident that they do not lie about the abuse they have suffered. All the stories I have shared are in sync with other stories the children have told. Sometimes a child independently has told a story to a volunteer and to me. We also check with others who know the child. I have not told the worst stories, nor have I explained the magnitude of the abuse the children have suffered. We have observed behaviors that support reports of widespread sexual abuse.

Once you get to know the children you get the feeling for what they will lie about and what they won't. Generally, they feel embarrassed about physical and sexual abuse and are hesitant to tell it until they know you are a person who can be trusted. Once I asked a boy about the cut on his cheek and the black eye. He just shrugged it off as an everyday occurrence. Later, I learned a staff person hit him. We must not only listen to what they say, but also to how they act. When a child flinches as you reach to touch his shoulder, you know he has been hit.

Q: Can the teen orphans get the therapy they need for healing in Romania?

A. The type of therapy post institutional children need is not easy to find even in the US. It is rarely available in Romania because few therapists are trained in the area of bonding and attachment. This is a field that has only fully developed in the last twenty years in the west. Many therapists do not understand the multitude of needs an orphan presents. This understanding will come as more Romanians are educated in these areas.

Q: What are the penalties for those who abuse children?

A. There is a law in Romania against abusing children residing in out-of-home placements. In the future, I believe Child Protection will pay more attention to the care these children receive. Some abusive caregivers have lost their jobs, while others have been penalized with loss of pay. I am not aware of criminal penalties.

Q: What social services are available for young, pregnant women?

A. In the Gypsy communities there are few social services, and there is no safety net such as housing for the homeless. Some nongovernment organizations provide housing and other assistance for women who have nowhere to go. More and more Gypsies are becoming believers, and many churches have been started. These churches are very poor, but some are providing help with health care and nutrition.

Q: Are churches more involved in advocacy and ministry to the orphans?

A. In general, most village churches do not have the resources to assist the orphans with special programs. However, there are churches that welcome the children in church services. FCE provides a Bible study and an evening of worship each week.

Q: What about children with special needs? Are they receiving better care today?

A. The care of handicapped children in institutions should be improved. These children have few activities and often have nothing to do to pass the time. For handicapped children in families, we know of both public and private schools in Oradea and Bucharest. It is very unusual for a small town to have a school such as the special school in Marghita started by FCE.

Both Lavinia and Silvia have their own special home. Casa Alba is home to six children all of whom are hard to place children. Silvia will need care all of her life due to her limitations. However, she is charming, fun-loving, and especially good at singing. An American volunteer, Brenda, who is an occupational therapist, supervises their care. The girls learn practical skills like setting the table and cooking. They attend FCE's school for special needs children.

Q: Do you see any improvement in Romania?

A. Since our first years in Romania, we have seen many improvements. The infrastructure of the country is changing every day. I only know the area of Bihor, but we see improvements every month. When we first came, there were no streetlights anywhere, and now even the villages have them. People struggle to provide necessities for their families, especially those living in villages, because income cannot keep up with inflation. Food and utilities are expensive and take a large percentage of a worker's wages.

Q: How has Romania's entry into the European Union affected the children?

A. The impact of the EU is a question for everyone. Hopefully it will raise the standard of child care in all sectors.

Q: Is discrimination against Gypsies continuing?

A. I would say that some degree of discrimination continues against minorities by the majority. Gypsies do not have the same rights and protections as Romanians. They do not have the same opportunities for education and jobs. Romania is not alone in this struggle for equality. With a new generation, I hope to see more Gypsies in leadership roles.

Q: Are Romanian families willing to adopt or foster the orphans?

A. Yes, some have adopted and others are foster parents. The interest is increasing, and this is encouraging. However, some of the children are not legally free for adoption. Older children are often very difficult to place and often do not adjust well in a family environment.

Q. How many volunteers are ministering under FCE?
A. The number varies, but usually is around twenty-five. We have teams coming to run the camps in the summer. Also, we have large Swedish construction crews that come and stay several weeks.

Q: Are more of the orphanage staff getting training in the care of children?
A. Child Protection provides training and so do NGO's (nongovernment organizations). University degree programs in social work and psychology will prepare professionals to train more caregivers.

Q: Will the orphanages be closed?
A. Romania is moving in that direction. It is expensive to run an institution, and I believe the new wave of the future for abandoned children will be smaller group homes. There is a population of disabled children and young people who will need some form of care with trained caregivers for the rest of their lives.

Q. Do you feel safe in Romania?
A. I feel safer in Marghita than in the suburbs of Denver. The greatest dangers here are the highways with impatient drivers who drive too fast. Most roads are two lane. A four lane highway is being built from Budapest, Hungary, to Brasov in central Romania.

Q. What is your primary ministry in Marghita?
A. Fred and I minister to the older teens by offering classes in English and building relationships with them. Fred is responsible for the team of volunteers who reach out to orphans in nearby state institutions and in the transit homes. Also, Fred and I oversee the Family Friends sponsorship program for the children placed by FCE in foster homes and the transit homes. We are mentors for the FCE team of volunteers. From time to time, I continue to teach FCE staff and volunteers about the special needs of orphans. Fred serves on FCE's board of directors.

Q: How long do you plan to live in Romania?
A. Fred and I are retired now and will live in Romania as long as we are in good health or until we are no longer needed here.

Q. What has inspired you the most during your ministry in Romania?
A. When a child is placed in a family and all are adjusted and happy. It is wonderful to see a child receiving good care and the love of a mother and father.

*Fred and I are retired now
and will live in Romania
as long as we are in good health
or until we are
no longer needed here.*

Barbro, Silvia, and Lars

The Glass Between Us

by Mary Dewey

The heat rises from the streets of Delhi, stirring the woman's sari. She is crying, distraught, her hands pressed against the glass of our car window. She holds something up for me to see; it looks like a hospital bill. Her hand slams desperately, again and again, making smudges on the glass. I look away, telling myself there is nothing I can do. The traffic light turns green, and the sound of dozens of motorcycles revving their engines drowns out the woman's cries. We leave her behind in a cloud of exhaust. But she follows me, out of the alleys filled with animal refuse, past the garbage heaps and ragged children. She follows me beneath the bright fluorescent lights of the airport, across the dark ocean, and into another country far away.

Light filters down through the trees of the Romanian forest, in through the car window smeared with handprints and tears. The cries are on my side of the glass this time. They come from a boy with curly black hair who clutches my hand as if I was saving him from drowning. For him and the other orphans packed beside him in the van, this trip marks the end of a week of summer camp.

We wind through the countryside, jolting over unpaved roads toward the orphanage where he will spend the rest of the year. The gray concrete building looms ahead of us, shutting out the light of the setting sun. As the van pulls up, children pour out of the orphanage doors and mob us. The boy climbs out of the van, wiping away the tears so the other children won't see that he has been crying. I hug him good-bye, and then a little girl, and then a different boy, and then someone I don't recognize. Hands cling to mine as I shut the sliding door. They press against the glass and trace hearts on the windows, and the children are running, running after us as we drive away.

I stare into the dusk through the hand-smudged glass. I remember the Indian woman, the woman who I told myself I could not help. I knew that if I rolled down the window, I would be torn to pieces by all the desperation. It's too much for one person, too much for a million people even if there were a million people willing to give themselves to heal these wounds. But my hands remember the feeling of that boy's hand in mine. There was no glass to protect me from his need, no glass to keep the heat and filth from my air-conditioned world. I was broken then, drowned. The flood poured out of my eyes as we pulled away.

What is the glass? It cleaves the world in two, gives comfort to the lucky few who were born on the right side. I stare down at my hands, hands that were afraid to touch the Indian woman's for fear that if they did, my world would be shattered. I remember the boy's hands and I know that I will come back next summer, hold his hands again, and be broken again. I will shatter the glass that stands between us and dive into the flood.

Karleen & Josif
at Casa Alba

Wanda Roberts &
baby at Casa Alba

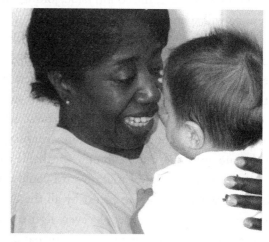

Lessons Learned From Abandoned Children

by Barb Demolar

In the first hours of meeting these children, especially for the first time, you are assaulted by sights, sounds, and smells that are out of your normal comfort zone. In the clamor for your attention, they poke, slap, kick, punch, and bite. Of course, it is all accompanied by a smile and the word "joke." However, the pain in your body and your astonished mind may not call it fun! The children have no sense of personal space and are in your face, dogging your every step. They are quick to pick up and point out anything about you . . . freckles, gray hair, extra weight, a crooked finger, some other anomaly. You can only hope that the words you don't understand are not too offensive.

You become acutely aware, in the days you spend with them, that they are consumed with survival. They are totally absorbed in their own needs, wondering when they will eat again, what they will do with their time, what gifts you will give them, and if you are prepared to be completely at their disposal. They are unabashed in their requests, willing to do whatever is necessary to achieve their desires. For some, this may involve lying, stealing, or hurting another person to get what they want.

It can offend the sensibilities of those who have come to help. We want them to be grateful rather than greedy. We want them to be more sensitive to our needs, eager to get to know us, ready to learn from us. Some of them are this way, others are not. We have our favorites, and sometimes find it difficult to tolerate the less lovable.

Then the Holy Spirit draws back the veil from the eyes of our hearts. He shows us how much we are like these children. He doesn't see the difference. He reveals our grasping self-absorption, the times we find it impossible to trust Him and take matters into our own hands to get what we desire. He shows us some of the empty things we pursue when He is offering us all of His treasures in the heavenly places. He nudges us, or strongly convicts us, for our ingratitude for all He has given us. How often have we been consumed with our own needs and failed to see the pain of others? How many times have we been angry with a person or situation rather than gracious? Inconsiderate, rather than kind? Perhaps we have learned to hide the unacceptable because we are adults and our culture and environment dictates our behavior as surely as the orphanage does for these children. Yet God knows what a long way we have to go to become more like Him.

There are more lessons to be learned from the children. Suffering is a daily companion with whom they walk hand in hand. How incomprehensible this is to us. We fight against such a companion, demanding happiness, health, and fulfillment as our rights. These children die to themselves daily when there is not enough to eat; when their few possessions are taken from them; when they are physically, sexually, and emotionally abused. They rarely allow themselves the luxury of tears. It is a sign of weakness that is quickly used against them. We cannot begin to know how to die to self as they do.

Trust is another lesson learned. These children trust us with their secrets, share their pain, somehow know they are loved, and hold us so hard they nearly melt into us. We find it hard to trust that quickly or to let our guard down with others and with the Lord.

They have another lesson to teach us. They have had to learn to live for today. For so many of them, the future is a question mark, something to be feared. So they live in the now, enjoying the moment of laughter, of time spent with us, of learning, or whatever else they are experiencing. We need to learn to live NOW, not always thinking of what is next. God has so much for us in the NOW.

God revealed to me His delight in these precious treasures. His pleasure in the simplicity of their love, their willingness to wring the most out of the relationships and experiences they have. He lingers over the prayer of their longing hearts and savors each tear they shed in their heavy burden of grief. His heart breaks with their pain.

I am driven to my knees to plead for a greater capacity for love, for a willingness to go beyond the boundaries I have set around myself. I beg God for the desire and persistence to storm the gates of heaven for every precious heart. I thank Him for reminding me that He loved me when I was unlovable, for adopting me into His family, for giving me all of the treasures of heaven. I return home no longer content with who I was or what I have. I resolve never to forget the lessons learned from the children.

Gypsy Baptism

by Fred Dewey

"Look, here is water.
Why shouldn't I be baptized?"
Acts 8:37 NIV

We turned off the highway onto a path through a field. After bumping along for about 500 yards, we came to a compound of small houses, part of a Gypsy village not far from Bucharest. Two Romanian pastors, an American missionary and I, came to participate in the baptism of new believers in this village.

Riding in the car from Bucharest, I listened to the story of God's transforming work among these people during the past few months. Campus Crusade workers came to the village and presented the gospel using the *Jesus* film. Hundreds of villagers viewed the film which was shown on two occasions a few weeks apart. After the second showing, dozens of people prayed to accept Christ's invitation to come to Him for forgiveness of their sins and to accept His promise of a new life and everlasting hope. With the help of Romanian pastors, a church was started in the village, and the new believers wanted to be baptized.

After some discussion with the church and village leaders, a crowd formed and moved across the field to an irrigation ditch about 300 yards away. Before leaving the compound, some people slipped into white hospital coats. I guessed they were among those to be baptized. As we approached the ditch, people were coming from all directions, and in a few minutes several hundred people had gathered along the banks to watch. The ditch was about 20 feet wide, and when the pastors entered the murky water, I could see that it was chest deep. Those to be baptized stood near a large pipe that carried the ditch water under a small road. One by one, they climbed down from the pipe into the muddy water.

The first to be baptized was a large, dark-skinned man with a long handle-bar mustache and a broad smile on his face. I was told he was the first man in the village to respond to the invitation to accept Christ. He also had been the most notorious thief and cheat in the area—before his life was transformed. He was big and tough, and he didn't hesitate to justify his reputation with his fists. Now, he raised those hands toward heaven and praised God for the joy, peace, and hope that he had received.

In Romanian, one of the pastors spoke the powerful words, "I baptize you in the Name of the Father, the Son, and the Holy Spirit."

Down under the water he went, then was raised in victory. The water was filthy, but this man who had been washed clean by the blood of Christ was triumphant. His beaming smile and torrent of tears said it all. The crowd cheered and enthusiastically sang a hymn.

And so it went—for more than three hours! Forty people were baptized that day—boys and girls, men and women, and old folks wrinkled with the years. Each one in a white coat, many with tears streaming down their faces, testified at length and praised God for their new life and for His work in their hearts. Down they went to symbolize their sins washed away; up they were raised in victory and freedom from their bondage to sin and death. The applause of the crowd, the singing of a hymn, was repeated again and again.

Have I ever witnessed such an incredible testimony of the transforming power of God? I cannot find words to express how grateful and privileged I felt to share this experience with these special people. These who were outcasts were welcomed by the King of kings!

"See that you do not look down on one of these little ones.
For I tell you that their angels in heaven always see
the face of my Father in heaven."
Matthew 18:10 NIV

God's Balance

by Phyllis Parker

Have you counted the cost?" Those preparing for the mission field are often asked this question. Others make the statement, "You sure are giving up a lot to go over there."

Somehow going on the mission field seems like gain minus loss equals the direction we should go. If the loss is greater than the gain, than it is reasoned that martyrdom is imminent. It is assumed that your desire to serve God is superior to others. After all, you are willing to endure the hardships of the mission field.

When the balance scale tips toward the loss side, maybe my ministry plans should be reevaluated? If the scale tips toward gain, then it is God's will for me to go.

But this evaluation of a ministry plan where "gain minus loss equals the degree of success" is not God's way. God doesn't do His business that way. He is only interested in gains that are eternally significant. Whether it is gain or loss, the scale is always tipped toward gain. That's God's balance.

I'll tell you my story. The following summer after my husband died, I needed to do something different. I decided to travel with Friendship International to see the needs in Romania. We heard that an orphanage in Ocna Mures needed shoes. We took four suitcases of shoes for the children. One day, we went to the patio area of an apartment with no windows and doors. Our group sang, did skits, and handed out pamphlets written in Romanian telling of the love of Jesus. People packed that place. We saw the real hopelessness in their eyes. These were jobless people without food and not even bathing facilities. The salt mines in this area were shut down, and the employment was only 10 percent of what it had been previously. Yet I was encouraged because a pastor and his wife had started an orphanage. They took in abandoned babies from the state run orphanage. Also, they spent time with young girls in the orphanage who the director used like prostitutes. The director allowed us to give only a short program in the orphanage.

All too soon, it was time to fly home. My heart was broken. On the plane, I prayed that God would use me in some way to help the orphans.

Note: After Phyllis' first visit to Romania, she made several visits to Marghita with the Loving Arms team. Phyllis lived in Marghita for three years. She gave two young men, Imi and Koli, the gift of becoming skilled hairstylists. She describes her time in Romania as "pure gold."

Recommended Reading

A Tearful Celebration—Finding God in the Midst of Loss by Dr. James Means.
Sisters, OR: Multnomah Press, 2006.

Abandoned for Life by Izidor Ruckel. St. Louis: JB Information Station, 2002.
http://www.abandonedforlife.com and http://www.EmpoweredParent.com

Bury Me Standing—The Gypsies and Their Journey by Isabel Fonseca.
New York: A.A. Knopf, 1995.

Children in Crisis: A New Commitment edited by Dr. Phyllis Kilbourn. MARC, 1996.

Don't Touch My Heart by Lynde Gainforte Mansfield, Christoper H. Waldmann.
Colorado Springs: NavPress, 1994.

Help for the Hopeless Child—A Guide for Families by Dr. Ronald S. Federici.
Alexandria, Virginia: Dr. Ronald Federici and Associates, 2003.

Instant Romanian for Parents and Caregivers by Teri Doolittle. 2006. www.lulu.com

The Natashas—Inside the New Global Sex Trade by Victor Malarek.
New York: Arcade, Time Warner Book Group, 2004.

Too Small to Ignore—Why Children Are the Next Big Thing by Dr. Wess Stafford.
Colorado Springs, CO: WaterBrook Press, 2005.

Parenting with Love and Logic by Foster Cline and Jim Fay.
Golden, CO: Love and Logic Press, 1997.

Uncontrollable Kids—from Heartbreak to Hope by Foster W. Cline.
Golden, CO: Love and Logic Press, 2001.

When Love is Not Enough by Nancy L. Thomas.
Glenwood Springs, CO: Families By Design, 1997.

How You Can Help

Thank you for reading *The Place of the Mourning Doves*. I deeply appreciate your interest in the orphans of Romania. All of the proceeds from the sale of this book will go to Fundatia Crestina Elim (FCE) in Marghita, Romania, to continue the work of bringing hope to abandoned children in Romania. I would be grateful if you would encourage others to purchase their own copy of the book.

Family Friends is a sponsorship program to financially support the orphans as they are placed in foster families or transit homes. Further information on sponsoring a child can be found on the web page of Mercy Ministries, www.mercymins.org. Questions may be directed to mercymins@msn.com.

The work of FCE with Romanian orphans depends upon the financial support of many generous people. If you cannot sponsor a child but you would like to give, you may do so through the Mercy Ministries Web site or by mailing a check to the address given below. You will receive a tax deductible receipt for your donation. Thank you for your part in bringing hope to the abandoned children of Romania.

For those who may be interested in volunteering with FCE in Marghita or for further information about the ministries of the foundation, please see the FCE web page, www.fce.org.

Copies of this book can be ordered online through Mercy Ministries or by US mail. When ordering by mail, please enclose a money order or your personal check payable to Mercy Ministries for the price of the book ($15.95) plus shipping and handling ($3.00), and sales tax if applicable. For information on quantity discounts, contact Mercy Ministries.

Mercy Ministries of Colorado

Mercy Ministries
5610 Ward Rd, Suite 110
Arvada, CO 80002
www.mercy-ministries.com
Email: mercymins@msn.com

A Word from the Publisher

On another cold day in March of 1998 I pause to sit on a rusty bench in the courtyard outside the pediatric section of the hospital in Marghita, Romania. I am drawn again and again to this place where it all began many years ago. High above, doves perched on bare branches silhouette against the sky. I struggle with my emotions as I hear their somber call. To me, they are mourning for the lost children who are imprisoned inside the hospital. "Cooo, Cooo, Cooo." Now, whenever I hear that poignant sound, my thoughts return to my first encounter with Romanian orphans.

Two years ago I read the above words for the first time at the Colorado Christian Writers Conference. Immediately they captured my heart. "This book needs to be published," I told Karleen.

I'm praying *The Place of the Mourning Doves* will impact you as powerfully as it has me. Show us, Father, how You are calling each one of us to reach out to hurting children around the world and in our own backyard. Open our eyes, reorder our priorities, and stretch our faith to believe that empowered by Your Spirit we really can make a difference.

Marlene Bagnull
Publisher and Editor
Ampelos Press
316 Blanchard Road
Drexel Hill, PA 19026
www.writehisanswer.com